Keepsakes

by Pat Cook

Single copies of plays are sold for reading purposes only. The copying or duplicating of a play, or any part of play, by hand or by any other process, is an infringement of the copyright. Such infringement will be vigorously prosecuted

Baker's Plays
7611 Sunset Blvd.
Los Angeles, CA 90042
bakersplays.com

NOTICE

This book is offered for sale at the price quoted only on the understanding that, if any additional copies of the whole or any part are necessary for its production, such additional copies will be purchased. The attention of all purchasers is directed to the following: This work is protected under the copyright laws of the United States of America, in the British Empire, including the Dominion of Canada, and all other countries adhering to the Universal Copyright Convention. Violations of the Copyright Law are punishable by fine or imprisonment, or both. The copying or duplication of this work or any part of this work, by hand or by any process, is an infringement of the copyright and will be vigorously prosecuted.

This play may not be produced by amateurs or professionals for public or private performance without first submitting application for performing rights. Royalties are due on all performances whether for charity or gain, or whether admission is charged or not Since performance of this play without the payment of the royalty fee renders anybody participating liable to severe penalties imposed by the law, anybody acting in this play should be sure, before doing so, that the royalty fee has been paid. Professional rights, reading rights, radio broadcasting, television and all mechanical rights, etc. are strictly reserved. Application for performing rights should be made directly to BAKER'S PLAYS.

No one shall commit or authorize any act or omission by which the copyright of, or the right to copyright, this play may be impaired. No one shall make any changes in this play for the purpose of production.

Publication of this play does not imply availability for performance. Both amateurs and professionals considering a production are strongly advised in their own interest to apply to Baker's Plays for written permission before starting rehearsals, advertising, or booking a theatre.

Whenever the play is produced, the author's name must be carried in all publicity, advertising and programs. Also, the following notice must appear on all printed programs, "Produced by special arrangement with Baker's Plays."

Licensing fees for *KEEPSAKES* is based on a per performance rate and payable one week in advance of the production.

Please consult the Baker's Plays website at www.bakersplays.com or our current print catalogue for up to date licensing fee information.

Copyright © 2008 by Pat Cook
Made in U.S.A.
All rights reserved.

KEEPSAKES
ISBN 978-0-87440-188-2
#1809-B

CHARACTERS

AUSTIN ROGERS – Laid back and amiable Father, around 50.
MARY JO ROGERS – Optimistic Mother in her late 40's.
PAWPAW KENDEROW – Eccentric grandfather, around 80.
BRENDA SORRELL – MARY JO'S spoiled sister, around 50.
DALE SORRELL – BRENDA'S long suffering husband, also around 50.
VAL PERSKY – Sister to MARY JO and BRENDA, in her 50's.
MITCHELL ROGERS – 22 year old son, bright and friendly.
JAN ROGERS – sassy 14 year old daughter.
TISH LAWRENCE – MITCHELL'S fiancé, early 20's.
LORI KENDEROW – PAWPAW'S late wife, in her 40's.

TIME

The Present

PLACE

The Living Room of MARY JO'S and AUSTIN'S suburban house.

ACT ONE

"A day in the life..."

(The setting for this family portrait is the living room of the house belonging to **AUSTIN** *and* **MARY JO ROGERS**. *The room is warm and comfortably middle-class. After all, it's seen a lot of living. There are four doors utilized in the floor plan. The first, or 'Front', door is located SR which leads outside. There is a large picture window DS of the front door. The second door, located just right of USC, is a closet. The third door, located on the US wall, leads to the kitchen and subsequent dining room and the fourth door, SL, leads to the bedrooms.*

The furniture in the room is the usual assortment of pieces. The large, overstuffed couch is located just left of DSC, which has a long couch table directly behind it. There are also two end tables flanking it. Against the SL wall sits the entertainment center, complete with television and radio. A heavy recliner rests near the DSR area, facing the television, with a DS odd table at its arm. There is a writing desk and matching chair against the US wall, between the kitchen door and SR wall. A telephone and various framed family pictures, including a large one of **PAWPAW**, *rest on top of the desk. There is a camera with flash attachment, on a tripod, DSR, facing the group.*

At the beginning of the play the family is gathered on and around the couch, facing out. **PAWPAW** *is seated in the center of the couch. On one side of sits* **BRENDA** *and on the other sits* **MARY JO**. **VAL** *is sitting on a couch arm.* **JAN** *is leaning on a couch arm. Behind them stand* **MITCHELL, AUSTIN** *and* **DALE**.

The LIGHTS come up with a suddenness that causes the family to rub their eyes and complain.)

PAWPAW. What was that?!

DALE. Is that it?

VAL. This is SO dumb!

BRENDA. Did you get it, Mitch?

MITCHELL. Hang on. *(He rushes over to the camera and checks it.)*

VAL. I hope you didn't cut my head off again. What kind of a family picture would that be with my head cut off?

MARY JO. Don't everybody start complaining at once.

VAL. I just asked.

DALE. Are we going to eat today?

AUSTIN. Mitch?

MITCHELL. Let's get one more for insurance.

PAWPAW. Insurance? Who's selling insurance? Don't you let them in that door, you hear?

BRENDA. Nobody's selling insurance, Dad.

PAWPAW. I didn't get all dressed up just so you could get me to sign some insurance thing, I'm not stupid, you know.

BRENDA. We're not selling you ANYthing, Dad!

PAWPAW. Better not.

VAL. He just says things like that to rile you.

BRENDA. I know, I know! *(She glares at her father.)* And it works every time! *(Unseen by **BRENDA**, **PAWPAW** laughs quietly to himself.)*

MARY JO. He just wants to take another PICTURE for INSURANCE, Dad.

PAWPAW. Who?

DALE. Mitchell! *(He points at his son.)* Your grandson!

PAWPAW. Mitchell?

MITCHELL. Here, sir.

PAWPAW. You're selling insurance now?

VAL. Let GO of it, Dad! He's NOT selling insurance!

MARY JO. He just wants to make sure we have a good photo of the whole family.

PAWPAW. Who?

DALE. I TOLD you to wait until he was asleep and then take the picture.

BRENDA. You're not helping, dear.

MITCHELL. Okay. And... *(He pushes a button on the camera and moves to his original position.)* Everybody smile?

AUSTIN. I thought you wanted us to be natural?

MARY JO. Austin?

AUSTIN. Sorry.

JAN. Let's just get THROUGH this, CAN we?

MARY JO. That's not a very helpful attitude, young lady.

MITCHELL. Everybody? Look at the camera!

*(Everyone, except for **PAWPAW**, looks at the camera and smiles. And smiles. And smiles.)*

PAWPAW. *(After the pause.)* What're we waiting for?

AUSTIN. Did you set it right, Mitchell?

MITCHELL. Yes, Dad.

PAWPAW. I have to go to the can. *(He gets to his feet.)*

VAL. Dad!

JAN. Pawpaw, don't!

*(**PAWPAW** turns his back to the camera to face the others.)*

PAWPAW. What? *(The flash goes off. The others moan and get disgusted looks on their faces. **PAWPAW** turns to **MITCHELL**.)* What was that?

MITCHELL. *(Adjusting the camera.)* That was me getting a good picture of your back, Pawpaw.

PAWPAW. Why'd you want a picture of my back?

MITCHELL. I didn't say I WANTED one but that's what I got.

MARY JO. Mitch, I'm sure that first one took.

*(**PAWPAW** moves to the SL door. The others relax and begin to move around.)*

MITCHELL. When Tish gets here I want another one with all of us.

DALE. Are we going to eat THEN?

BRENDA. Yes, dear.

DALE. I am starving to death. *(He rubs his chest with two fingers.)* Here, feel my backbone.

PAWPAW. And when I get back I want you two to help me get my trunk outta' the cellar.

AUSTIN. Which two? *(He catches himself and slaps a hand over his mouth.)*

PAWPAW. You and Dale.

DALE. He's not here.

PAWPAW. Who said that?

BRENDA. Dale.

DALE. *(To* **BRENDA.***)* That's it; you're out of my will.

PAWPAW. I thought so!

JAN. *(Moves next to* **PAWPAW.***)*

I'll help you, Pawpaw.

PAWPAW. At least ONE member of this family ain't afraid of a little work. *(He looks at her.)* Who are you, again?

JAN. Pawpaw!

PAWPAW. *(Playfully hugs her.)* Oh, JanJan, I was just ribbin' you.

JAN. Ribbin' me? What's THAT mean?

VAL. It's an old phrase, dear. Dad's full of them.

MARY JO. It means he's kidding you. I think ribbing you is one of those sayings, isn't it, that came from Adam? *(She looks at* **AUSTIN.***)* Getting a rib from Adam, that kind of thing.

JAN. Adam?!

BRENDA. Yes. He and your grandfather grew up together.

PAWPAW. Hey! *(He points a finger at* **BRENDA.***)* He taught me ever'thing I know! *(To himself.)* This family, I swear… *(He exits out the SL door.)*

JAN. Can I go to my room now?

MARY JO. No! How often to we get the family together? And you want to go hide in your room?

JAN. Mom! I KNOW what they look like! Gah!

MITCHELL. Okay, folks, now look. *(The group starts chatting among themselves.)*

AUSTIN. *(To **MARY JO**.)* What's he want us to move that old trunk of his for?

MARY JO. I don't know, it's the first I've heard of it.

AUSTIN. Well, he's your father.

DALE. *(Same time as **AUSTIN**.)* Did you bring my cell phone?

BRENDA. Yes. You left it on the bed and I KNEW you'd want it so I put it in my purse.

VAL. *(Same time as **DALE**.)* You know, I've always wondered what the old man has kept in that trunk of his.

MITCHELL. Everybody? Hello!

MARY JO. *(Waves at the others.)* Okay, y'all? *(The others get quiet.)* Mitchell wants our attention.

MITCHELL. No big deal. And let's don't make this into a big deal. When Tish gets here? Everybody try to behave.

AUSTIN. What do you mean, son? *(He sticks a finger up his nose. **DALE** makes a face.)*

MITCHELL. *(Moves to his father.)* Well, she hasn't met most of you –

DALE. Then why're you bringing her over here?

MITCHELL. Not my idea. *(**MITCHELL**, **AUSTIN** and **JAN** look at **MARY JO**.)*

MARY JO. *(After a slight pause.)* Well?!

MITCHELL. Just behave, that's all I ask. Try to think of somebody normal and act like them.

JAN. Like we know anybody that's normal.

AUSTIN. I like to think we're a fairly normal American family.

DALE. Yeah?

AUSTIN. I LIKE to think that...

VAL. SAAAAY, let's bring out the family album!

MITCHELL. See?! That's EXACTLY what we don't want to do!

MARY JO. *(Moves to* **MITCHELL.***)* What's wrong with that?

MITCHELL. Mom, you know what always happens when we do that?

JAN. Not anymore. I ripped out that shot of me dressed up as a Martian.

AUSTIN. You were Trick or Treating!

JAN. Yes and it was in November!

MARY JO. You were sick during Halloween that year.

JAN. To this day, old Mrs. Patterson calls me 'that thing from outer space'.

AUSTIN. I don't think that has anything to do with that costume, hon.

JAN. It HAS to be.

AUSTIN. Old Mrs. Patterson didn't move here until 6 years ago.

JAN. Well, then why does Old Mrs. Patterson call me that then?

MARY JO. Don't call her 'old,' Jan. *(A slight pause.)* And besides, I showed her the family album.

JAN. See?!

MARY JO. Well, if you tore up that picture, young lady, you're grounded for a month!

JAN. Ohp! *(She kicks the floor.)*

MARY JO. None of that now. Let's all focus on what's important here.

AUSTIN. Right. I don't what to have to lug that heavy old trunk out of the basement and I don't care who knows it.

DALE. I'll help you.

AUSTIN. Don't volunteer, will you? Trust me on this one. Around here you never volunteer.

VAL. *(In a quieter tone.)* How IS Dad these days, anyway? *(She indicates the SL door.)*

MARY JO. *(Moves to* **VAL.***)* He's fine. He's slowing down a bit. That's to be expected

VAL. Not being just a tad optimistic, are you Mary Jo.

BRENDA. You were always the 'Pollyanna' in the family.

JAN. Does anyone in this family use language that was invented in this century? Who's 'Pollyanna'?

MITCH. Was that a car driving up? *(He moves to the window and looks out.)*

AUSTIN. She was a character in a movie. And played by Hayley Mills.

JAN. Who's HAYLEY MILLS?!

MARY JO. Lower your voice, Jan.

BRENDA. Austin, how is Dad really?

(AUSTIN starts to speak but then looks at MARY JO, who is watching him intently.)

AUSTIN. He's… slowing down a little.

VAL. Nice reading. *(To MARY JO.)* Did you two rehearse this act before we all got here?

MARY JO. What're you trying to stir up?

BRENDA. Mary Jo, will you tell us the truth! We're not blind, you know.

JAN. *(Moves to BRENDA and VAL.)* There's NOTHIN' wrong with Pawpaw!

(MITCHELL turns away from the window.)

MITCHELL. He is talking to himself a lot more.

VAL. I was afraid of that.

MARY JO. So? EVERYbody talks to themselves.

AUSTIN. Hon?

MARY JO. *(Moves to AUSTIN.)* Oh, and I suppose you don't talk to yourself?

AUSTIN. She just wants to know about her own father.

MARY JO. Answer me. You don't talk to yourself?

AUSTIN. No!

MARY JO. Yeah? What about when you're late coming home? You don't go over what you're going to tell me? You don't practice that in the car?

AUSTIN. Well – *(DALE laughs at this.)*

(MARY JO turns and moves to DALE.)

MARY JO. And you! After Brenda carps at you for being a slob, you don't mutter something vicious where she can't hear you?

DALE. No habla Englais.

MARY JO. S'what I thought. *(She turns and sees BRENDA glaring at her.)* What?

BRENDA. *(Evenly.)* I do NOT carp.

AUSTIN. Well, in any case, Pawpaw covers it up pretty well if you know what to look for.

DALE. What do you mean?

AUSTIN. Now when he talks to himself he snaps his fingers. *(DALE looks at his curiously.)* That way when anybody catches him they'll think he's singing.

JAN. I taught him that.

DALE. *(Looks at BRENDA.)* So we're going to eat today?

BRENDA. Soon!

DALE. Can I, at least, get a roll?

BRENDA. You start with me today, Dale Meredith Sorrell, and I'll lay into you until who laid the rails! *(She looks at JAN, who's staring at her.)* That's another old – never mind.

MARY JO. *(Moves to MITCHELL.)* When did Tish say she'd be here? *(She looks at the others.)* She said, trying to change the subject.

MITCHELL. *(Looks at his watch.)* Ten minutes ago. She's usually very punctual.

DALE. That'll be the first thing to go.

MITCHELL. What?

DALE. After you two get married.

MITCHELL. We're not engaged… yet. We're engaged to be engaged.

AUSTIN. Now you KNOW that concept was thought up by a woman.

JAN. This is SO lame! *(She exits out the SL door.)*

MARY JO. Don't get on the phone! Tish may try to call and she won't get through if – (**JAN** *has exited.* **MARY JO** *looks at the others.*) Are they blessings, though?

DALE. *(Moves to* **MITCHELL.***)* You WILL talk to us before you take the plunge, right?

MITCHELL. Talk to who?

DALE. Me and your old Dad here.

AUSTIN. Don't get me in this.

BRENDA. And just what're you going to tell him, dear? *(Wolfish grin.)*

DALE. Just a few facts. *(To* **MITCHELL,** *as he counts on his fingers.)* One, you're always hungry –

BRENDA. All RIGHT! *(To her sisters.)* Let's get the food on the table before he starts harping on marriage.

VAL. You two are SO perfect for each other; I've always thought that.

BRENDA. That's the nastiest thing you've ever said to me.

MARY JO. You haven't been listening. (**VAL** *turns to her.*) I need to check on the roast, anyway. *(She moves US.)*

VAL. And then we can REALLY talk! *(She looks at the men.)*

BRENDA. And maybe Mary Jo will tell us the truth about Dad.

*(***MARY JO*** starts to speak but changes her mind and then enters the kitchen door.)*

VAL. *(To* **BRENDA.***)* Just keep picking at it, why don't you?

BRENDA. Like you don't want to know yourself.

VAL. Yes but I – oh, never mind! *(She and* **BRENDA** *exit through the kitchen door.)*

DALE. Is the old man really getting bad?

AUSTIN. I can't... I really shouldn't say.

DALE. He's almost eighty, it's not surprising. *(A cell phone rings.)*

MITCHELL. Somebody's cell phone.

DALE. Yeah, that's mine. *(He moves to the couch table where there are three purses.)*

AUSTIN. Has your mother said anything to you about him?
MITCHELL. About Pawpaw?
AUSTIN. Yeah.

(DALE opens a purse and goes through it. He pulls all its contents out onto the table. Not finding anything he goes to the next one. This takes place during the next few speeches.)

MITCHELL. You know Mom. She plays 'em close to the vest.

AUSTIN. Probably better that way.

MITCHELL. Why? Is he – Is there something I ought to know?

AUSTIN. You've seen everything we've seen. The talking to himself, late night walks, memory lapses. Sometimes he seems to grope for words... I don't know.

MITCHELL. You and Mom aren't thinking of putting him in a nursing home, are you?

AUSTIN. I thought about one of those assisted living places, you know? *(He looks through the drapes out the window.)* Brought it up a couple of times.

MITCHELL. Have you talked to Pawpaw about it?

AUSTIN. No, the first thing is to prepare your mother. She still sees him like when she was a teenager.

(DALE opens the next purse and takes items out of that one.)

MITCHELL. That's going to be hard. On all of us.

AUSTIN. I know, I know.

MITCHELL. Maybe it's his medication.

AUSTIN. Maybe. One more of those late night strolls of his –

DALE. Did anybody see which purse Brenda brought?

AUSTIN. What? *(The cell phone stops ringing as AUSTIN and MITCHELL turn to DALE.)*

DALE. Never mind. *(He moves to the others.)* Now. Just how serious is it?

AUSTIN. We haven't made any decisions yet, if that's what you mean.

DALE. I mean Mitch and What's-her-name?

MITCHELL. Not sure.

DALE. You don't know how you feel about her?

MITCHELL. No, I'm not sure I want to tell you guys.

AUSTIN. Smart. *(He looks at DALE.)* What's that phrase? That we're supposed to tell him?

DALE. You know it as well as I do.

DALE & AUSTIN. *(To MITCHELL.)* Marriage is a wonderful thing.

AUSTIN. But – *(He looks around and then back at MITCHELL)* – you make up your own mind. Marriage is a big step, it's a big responsibility. *(To DALE.)* What else?

DALE. Marriage consists in large part of just flat giving up.

AUSTIN. Don't tell him that!

DALE. Hey, I used to smoke cigars, go fishing every chance I got, wear whatever I wanted to, keep beer in the house and own a dog!

MITCHELL. And now?

(DALE shakes his head.)

AUSTIN. *(Trying to help.)* You still have the dog.

DALE. *(Bad taste in his mouth.)* Nah, she got that decorator dog, that Pomeranian! Charlemaine, is that a name for a dog? I tried to call him Charley – nothing. Doesn't come when you call him, NEVER been house-broken, just a little, fat, furry ball of – *(He illustrates with his hands.)*

(Just then PAWPAW enters through the SL door. AUSTIN sees him and grabs DALE's hands.)

AUSTIN. *(Loud whisper.)* Don't move!

DALE. *(Also whispering.)* What?

AUSTIN. Be still!

DALE. Huh? *(He turns and sees PAWPAW, who's looking around the room.)*

AUSTIN. *(After a slight pause.)* His vision is based on movement.

(DALE nods and the three men stand perfectly still. PAWPAW moves into the room, still looking for people.)

PAWPAW. Where'd everybody go? *(He moves closer to the trio and stops. He then sniffs the air, waits and sniffs it again. He moves away from them and DALE wipes his brow. Suddenly, PAWPAW turns back and again DALE freezes.)*

(MARY JO enters from the kitchen, followed by VAL and BRENDA.)

MARY JO. Can't you two talk about something else?

VAL. We're just trying to help, dear.

MARY JO. You want to help?

BRENDA. Yes! Isn't that what we've been saying?

MARY JO. Then you can – *(She sees the others.)* What ARE you people doing?

PAWPAW. Austin pulled that old gag that my vision is based on movement.

DALE. What?

(AUSTIN and MITCHELL laugh slightly. PAWPAW quickly turns to AUSTIN, who immediately stops laughing.)

AUSTIN. Pawpaw, I don't want to have to lug that old trunk upstairs and get all hot and sweaty –

VAL. *(Sees the purses.)* Who's been going through all our purses?

DALE. Brenda, just WHICH purse is yours? *(He moves to his wife.)*

BRENDA. What? *(She picks up the purse on the end.)* Cell phone rang, didn't it? *(She drops the purse and looks at her sisters.)* They NEVER notice anything, do they? I've owned this purse for years!

DALE. Just give me the phone.

BRENDA. Here! *(She opens her purse and hands him a cell phone.)*

MARY JO. Any news about Tish?

MITCHELL. Still waiting.

MARY JO. We'll wait lunch until she gets here.

DALE. Don't change the rules after the game started?! *(To the others.)* I don't know why I suited up for this.

VAL. Mary Jo, can we go back into the kitchen and –

MARY JO. NO! I'm sick and tired of talking about – *(She turns and looks at* **PAWPAW***, who doesn't see this.)*

BRENDA. You act like we're the enemy, like we're news reporters or something.

AUSTIN. What? What's going on now –

MARY JO. Don't ask.

BRENDA. That's what she told us.

MARY JO. Look! How often do we get the family together? Huh? And here it is, a sunny day, we're waiting to meet Mitch's girlfriend and all you want to do is argue! Well, we're going to have a good time today if it kills you all! *(She picks up the phone and practically yells into the receiver.)* Jan, get back in here and I mean right now! *(She puts the receiver down and stares at the others.)*

AUSTIN. *(After a pause.)* Sooooo…

VAL. *(Moves to* **MITCHELL***.)* Mitch, why don't you tell us all about Tish?

MARY JO. She's a sweet girl; don't start in on her.

BRENDA. How did you meet her?

MITCHELL. Well, –

DALE. Watch what you say, boy. *(He looks at his wife.)* They remember EVERYthing.

VAL. *(To* **AUSTIN***.)* And how about you?

AUSTIN. *(Gleefully.)* Yeah, how ABOUT me!

VAL. Have you and he – *(She nods toward* **MITCHELL***)* – you know, had the talk yet?

*(***AUSTIN*** thinks for a beat or two and turns to* **MITCHELL***.)*

AUSTIN. You know about sex, right?

MITCHELL. Yeah.

AUSTIN. Thank God.

(**JAN** *enters through the SL door.*)

JAN. Mom?! Have you totally lost it? I was talking to Junie. And do you know who wants to take me out on a date?

AUSTIN. You're not old enough – *(To* **MARY JO***)* – how old is she?

MARY JO. Fourteen.

AUSTIN. *(To* **JAN***.)* You're not old enough to date. *(As an afterthought to* **MARY JO***.)* I thought fourteen, I just wasn't sure.

DALE. Wait'll they ask you to pick out their handbag in a line-up.

JAN. Will you ever let me grow up? EVERYbody in my class is dating.

MARY JO. And if everybody in your class jumped off a cliff –

JAN. Is that another old saying?

MARY JO. Don't you take that tone with me, young lady.

JAN. Gah! I swear, Mom, you'd think I was six again and Mitch and I were still doing that mellerdrama skit for company.

BRENDA. *(Brightens.)* Oh, I remember that! That was hilarious!

VAL. Can you still do it?

BRENDA. I'd love to see it.

(**JAN** *slowly lowers her head, shoulders and upper body in a bow until her head hits the sofa table.*)

MARY JO. *(Trying not to smile.)* You brought it up.

(**JAN** *then looks up at the purses.*)

JAN. Who's been going through the purses?

(**MARY JO** *and* **VAL** *put their items back in their purses.*)

MITCHELL. Mom, I don't think –

AUSTIN. Oh, go ahead, we could use some entertainment.

DALE. Yeah, we're not doing anything else, like, say, eating.

JAN. *(Rises.)* I won't do it!

MITCHELL. Jan, they're just going to nag us until we do.

BRENDA. Pawpaw, you want to see the kids do the mellerdrama skit?

PAWPAW. Oh, I remember that! That was great! Lori used to love that.

MARY JO. That's right, Mom really got such a boot out of it. *(To* **JAN.***)* Hon?

JAN. Ohp! *(She stamps one foot. Then she moves to the front of the couch and* **MITCHELL** *joins her there.*

The rest of the family sit on the couch or stand near it. **PAWPAW** *remains standing near the recliner.)*

MITCHELL. Ready?

MARY JO. Go ahead.

MITCHELL. And curtain up!

*(***JAN** *puts both hands up to her face and looks out with a mournful look on her face.* **MITCHELL** *laughs a long, sinister laugh and then twirls an imaginary moustache on both sides with both hands. He twirls it to great length and some of the family giggle at this.)*

JAN. *(Flatly.)* Oh woe is me, woe it me.

VAL. We don't believe you.

*(***JAN** *shoot her a look and resumes her position, speaking now in a very dramatic tone.)*

JAN. Oh, WOE is ME! WOE is ME!

MITCHELL. Ah, dear Prunella, you will give me over your ranch or your hand in marriage! *(Another laugh.)*

JAN. Oh, will no one come to my rescue? Am I forsaken?

MITCHELL. You will vouchsafe your honor to my will.

JAN. *(Hand to her forehead.)* Never! I shall not be swayed by your brutish manner nor evil ways! You are a bounder and a bully!

MITCHELL. Bounder and bully; why can't I be just one and not the other? You've never seen me bound!

JAN. No, but I've heard your bull.

MITCHELL. You shall be mine! *(He grabs* **JAN** *by her throat.)* Do you hear me? Mine! All mine! *(He brings* **JAN** *to her knees, still choking her, and laughing menacingly.*

Just then, there is a knock at the front door. **PAWPAW** *opens it.)*

PAWPAW. Come in and leave all hope behind.

TISH. *(Enters.)* I am SO sorry I'm late. *(She moves over to the couch area.)* There was a wreck on Travis and I – *(She sees* **MITCHELL** *throttling* **JAN**.*)* Uhm… Am I interrupting anything?

(The whole family, except for **JAN** *and* **MITCHELL**, *burst out laughing at the LIGHTS black out.)*

Scene Two

(It is now 2 hours later and after everyone has finally had lunch. **PAWPAW** *is stretched out on the recliner and sound asleep.* **TISH** *is sitting on the couch, between* **MARY JO** *and* **VAL**. *They are going through the family album.* **BRENDA** *is looking over a couch arm at the photos and* **MITCHELL** *is leaning against the other couch arm.)*

MARY JO. And here's Mitch in his Boy Scout uniform.

TISH. Awww. *(Looks at* **MITCHELL**.*)* You were fat.

MITCHELL. That wasn't me.

MARY JO. Mitchell, it is so you.

MITCHELL. I mean I wasn't fat; the uniform was. I got that from some guy who quit the Scouts.

MARY JO. *(To* **TISH**.*)* And they made him Quartermaster for the whole troop.

MITCHELL. Well, they had to. The badge was already on the uniform.

TISH. What did you do? *(Ever so proper.)* As Quartermaster, what were your duties, sir? *(She salutes him.)*

MARY JO. He got to store and maintain all the equipment for the whole troop.

MITCHELL. Yeah. I kept the Coleman lantern.

*(***AUSTIN*** and ***DALE*** enter through the SL door.* ***DALE*** *is wiping his hands with a handkerchief.)*

AUSTIN. Well, it's in there. *(He yells.)* Pawpaw, your trunk —

BRENDA. Quiet! He's out. *(She nods toward the recliner.)* Which is a blessing.

DALE. Did I have any calls?

BRENDA. No, you didn't have any calls. What're you expecting?

DALE. Just the usual, dear. You know I have a couple of contracts I've been trying to close.

AUSTIN. More swamp land you're foisting off on some unsuspecting rubes?

DALE. Of course. *(Kidding.)* Hey, if it's good enough for all those crocodiles, it's good enough for my clientele.

(**AUSTIN** *leans over the couch to look at the album.*)

AUSTIN. Oh, now he's got clientele, excuse me. Clientele.

DALE. Yeah, that's a Latin word for 'gang-o-suckers.'

VAL. I'm sure.

BRENDA. *(To* **VAL.***)* He's kidding!

TISH. *(Indicates the album.)* Who's this?

VAL. Oh, that's Mother.

TISH. She's beautiful.

BRENDA. Yes. We take after her.

(**AUSTIN** *and* **DALE** *exchange looks.*)

DALE. *(Almost under his breath.)* But not close enough.

MITCHELL. Mom, where's their marriage certificate?

VAL. *(Amazed.)* You found that?

MARY JO. Hang on. *(She thumbs through the album and stops at a page.)* Here.

BRENDA. Will you LOOK at THAT?!

TISH. *(Reading.)* Abner Lloyd Kenderow and Loretta Jane Marcus.

MARY JO. And here's their wedding photo. *(She turns the page.)*

VAL. Where did you FIND all this?

MARY JO. Pawpaw just brought it out a couple of months ago.

TISH. Loretta, I've always liked that name.

BRENDA. Yeah, he called her Lori. *(They all look at* **PAWPAW** *just as he lets out a loud snore.)* And she called him 'Bear.'

VAL. Aren't they cute when they're asleep?

DALE. You should hear what he called his kids. *(He points at the sisters on the couch.)*

BRENDA. Or his sons-in-laws.

TISH. Bear?

BRENDA. He used to be grumpy.

MITCHELL. Well, enough of this. *(He stands up.)* Where's Jan? *(He moves to the SL door.)*

MARY JO. I'm sure she's on the phone again. Doesn't Mitch look like Pawpaw?

VAL. I've always thought he did.

MITCHELL. *(Calls out the SL door.)* Jan! I need you in here. Pronto!

AUSTIN. What do you want with Jan?

MITCHELL. Just want her in here, that's all.

TISH. So it was just you three girls? They didn't have any other children?

VAL. Nope, just us chickens.

BRENDA. Pawpaw would rather one of us had been a boy.

VAL. Or all of us. Anything but girls. *(Studiously, to BRENDA.)* Maybe we should've been chickens.

MARY JO. He couldn't have loved us more; you two behave.

(JAN enters through the SL door.)

JAN. What is all the noise? I'm trying to study.

(AUSTIN and MARY JO crane to look at their daughter.)

AUSTIN. *(Holds out a hand.)* I'm sorry I was looking for my daughter. And you are… ?

JAN. This family is SO embarrassing! *(To MITCHELL.)* What do you want?

MITCHELL. Just wanted you to see something. *(He moves in front of the couch.)*

BRENDA. Oh, you want the couch?

MITCHELL. No, no, just stay where you are.

AUSTIN. Why am I suddenly getting a cold chill down my spine?

MARY JO. *(Looks back at AUSTIN.)* I hope you haven't caught that bug that's going around.

AUSTIN. Not that kind of bug, dear?

MARY JO. What? *(She turns to see MITCHELL getting down on one knee.)*

MITCHELL. Patricia? *(He tries to get comfortable while dodging* **BRENDA***'s legs,)*

BRENDA. I can move – what're you –

MITCHELL. You're fine, you're fine.

TISH. Yeah?

> *(***MITCHELL*** holds out his hand and she puts her hand in his.)*

MARY JO. Oh my – !

MITCHELL. You and I have known each other for some time now and it has come to my attention that I love you very much.

TISH. *(Tearing up.)* Yes?

DALE. *(To* **AUSTIN***.)* He's uh, he's uh, he's uh –

AUSTIN. I can see!

VAL. Will you two shut UP?!

JAN. I don't believe this.

MITCHELL. And I want to spend the rest of my life with you. Will you do me the honor of marrying me?

(Everyone, except for **PAWPAW***, turn to look at* **TISH***.)*

TISH. Oh, this is so sudden! I… yes, I will!

*(***MITCHELL*** and* **TISH*** both jump to their feet and kiss. The others look on, stunned.)*

JAN. *(Breaking the long silence.)* This family is SO embarrassing.

(The couple break the kiss. **MITCHELL** *looks at the others.)*

MITCHELL. Well? Isn't anybody going to say anything?

BRENDA. One question. This isn't another one of those skits, is it?

TISH. No, it's for real. *(***MITCHELL*** hugs her.)* It BETTER be.

(The group starts speaking loudly all at once. The ladies on the couch jump to their feet. Those awake, except for **JAN** *and* **DALE***, move to the couple.)*

BRENDA. Then congratulations!

VAL. *(Same time as **BRENDA**.)* What a lovely surprise!

MARY JO. *(Same time as **BRENDA**.)* Why didn't you tell us you were going to do this today? *(She and **TISH** hug.)*

AUSTIN. *(Same time as **BRENDA**.)* Pull something like this, I don't believe it! *(He shakes **MITCHELL**'s hand vigorously.)*

*(All the commotion wakes **PAWPAW**.)*

PAWPAW. What… what? What's all the ruckus? *(He sits up.)*

DALE. Mitch is getting married.

PAWPAW. Huh?

DALE. Mitch! Married!

PAWPAW. How long was I asleep?

MARY JO. *(To **JAN**.)* Jan! Come hug your brother.

AUSTIN. And your soon-to-be new sister.

JAN. *(Not sure.)* I'm sorta' working up to that.

PAWPAW. All this noise, I swear. *(He gets to his feet.)*

MITCHELL. Pawpaw, I just proposed.

PAWPAW. Proposed what?

AUSTIN. Marriage, what else?

PAWPAW. Has she met the family yet?

MITCHELL. What?

PAWPAW. Marry her before she gets a load of this aggregation. She'll run for her life.

TISH. *(Moves to **PAWPAW**.)* It's too late, Pawpaw. Can I call you that?

PAWPAW. You can call me anything but collect and late for dinner.

VAL. *(To **JAN**.)* That's another old –

*(**JAN** is about to cry and bolts from the room out the SL door.)*

MARY JO. Oh, she'll be all right. Something like this takes getting used to.

AUSTIN. *(To **TISH**.)* And so do we. I hope you know what you're getting into.

TISH. I have a pretty good idea.

(**PAWPAW** *moves to the SL door and exits.*)

BRENDA. That was the loveliest proposal I ever saw.

DALE. Hey!

BRENDA. Oh, you want me to bring up YOUR proposal? *(To the others.)* Did I ever tell you that? He asked if I owned my own house and then proposed.

VAL. Wow, the pageantry of it all!

MITCHELL. Mom, I'm worried about Jan. She took it kinda' –

MARY JO. Don't concern yourself, you know her. Any way you would've broken it to her she'd have taken it the same way.

TISH. I hope she doesn't hate me.

AUSTIN. Oh, I'm sure she does. She hates all of us at one time or another.

MITCHELL. *(To* **TISH.***)* We better go.

VAL. You're leaving?

BRENDA. Just like that? Hit us with your best trick and no encore?

MITCHELL. We better go tell Tish's parents.

TISH. Ooh, right. *(They move to the front door.)*

MITCHELL. Tell you what. Let's do the same thing there. I'll get down on one knee, the whole thing.

TISH. *(To the others.)* But you can't tell them, all right?

VAL. Hey, we know how to keep secrets here. Like Brenda's cosmetic surgery.

BRENDA. I had a deviated septum!

(*The others move to the front door with the couple.*)

MARY JO. Hope it's not too much of a problem with them.

DALE. Yeah, let us know if they put up a struggle. Austin and I are great at lugging things into and out of cellars.

MITCHELL. I'll call as soon as I can. *(He leans over and kisses* **MARY JO** *on the cheek.)* I love you, Mom.

MARY JO. I know. We all love you, too. *(She smiles at* **TISH**.*)*

*(***TISH** *and* **MITCHELL** *exit and* **MARY JO** *closes the door. As soon as they leave, the sisters turn to* **MARY JO**.*)*

BRENDA. You poor woman!

MARY JO. They're too young to get married!

VAL. What're you going to do?!

MARY JO. She won't know anything about him, what to do when he gets a cold – he gets them all the time!

BRENDA. What does EITHER of them know about being married?

VAL. And she's still a child herself!

(At this moment, **PAWPAW** *enters through the SL door.)*

PAWPAW. Hey! *(Everyone turns to him.)* What's the idea of putting my trunk in my room? You trying to get me to move?!

(All stare at him, not knowing what to say, as the LIGHTS dim out.)

Scene Three

(It is now later that night. The LIGHTS are lower and **JAN**, *now in her pajamas and robe, is sitting in the recliner. She is writing in her diary. She writes for a bit and then* **PAWPAW** *looks in through the kitchen door.)*

PAWPAW. What's all that music in here?

JAN. Huh? I don't hear any music. And I'm in here.

PAWPAW. *(Trying to see.)* Jan? That you?

JAN. Yes, Pawpaw.

PAWPAW. You ought to be in bed. *(He starts to leave and then looks back in.)* You're my favorite, you know.

JAN. And you're mine, you old Bear.

*(***PAWPAW*** smiles and closes the door.* **JAN** *writes more in her diary.)*

AUSTIN. *(Offstage.)* Jan, are you in the living room?

JAN. No!

AUSTIN. Get to bed, will you, please?

JAN. In a minute! *(She speaks as she writes.)* "Today I have decided… to join the circus. I'm sure I will fit right in… after living in this sideshow… all my life." *(***MITCHELL*** enters through the front door, sees* **JAN** *and closes the door quietly.)* "I hope that… I am not overqualified… and also… that they have cable."

MITCHELL. *(Leans over her.)* And the boogie man'll get'cha! *(***JAN*** jumps.)* If you don't watch out.

JAN. *(After composing herself.)* Oh, you are so funny; let me write this down right now. *(She writes.)* "My brother is an idiot."

MITCHELL. *(Leans against the arm.)* You have to remind yourself of that?

JAN. You're right. *(She marks through the line and writes again.)* "My brother is STILL in idiot."

MITCHELL. So. How do you like Tish.

JAN. I've met her before, you know that. *(She tries to get up but* **MITCHELL** *pulls her back.)*

MITCHELL. Hang on. Now. What's going on?

JAN. Nothin'!

MITCHELL. Jan? You're acting like you did when I moved into my apartment last year.

JAN. Yeah, you didn't ask me about that either!

MITCHELL. Oh. I see. I guess I should've mentioned all this to you before… you know, today.

JAN. *(Mock surprise.)* You think?

MITCHELL. You know, we're not sure, after we get married, where we're going to live. My apartment or hers. *(He leans in.)* Maybe we'll just move back here to my old room.

JAN. That's MY ROOM! *(She sees he's kidding.)* Oh!

MITCHELL. Don't you like Tish?

JAN. Yes! *(She gets to her feet.)*

MITCHELL. Really? What'd you write in your diary about her?

JAN. None of your whiney business.

MITCHELL. Jan, have we ever kept secrets from each other?

JAN. Well, let's see. There's today, there's your apartment, there's the time Dad caught you and Tish on the couch.

MITCHELL. How'd you find out about that?!

JAN. *(Points a finger at him.)* Ah HA! I KNEW that's what happened.

MITCHELL. Oh, foul! Clipping. Below the knees.

JAN. Whatever.

MITCHELL. *(Moves to JAN.)* Look. We love each other very much, okay? *(JAN doesn't say anything.)* Okay, how about this? How about I tell you a secret and it'll just be between you and me, how's that?

(JAN shakes her head vigorously and then looks at MITCHELL.)

JAN. What is it?

(MITCHELL looks around. JAN looks around. Then MITCHELL leans in to her.)

MITCHELL. I had already asked Tish to marry me last week.

JAN. What?

MITCHELL. And she said yes then. But we figured the whole family would get such a charge out of seeing me propose here –

JAN. That is SO – *(She breaks into a wide smile)* – sneaky!

MITCHELL. *(Also with a wide smile.)* I know. I mean I wasn't going to take a chance that I'd ask her here, in front of God, the family and everybody, and have her say 'No,' right? Think how embarrassing THAT would've been?

JAN. Oh, right.

MITCHELL. And you'd have laughed.

JAN. Oh, I would've, too.

MITCHELL. Now. You better get to bed.

JAN. You sound like Dad now. I'm not sleepy and – **(MITCHELL** *snatches her diary away from her)* – Hey! Gimme' that!

MITCHELL. Will you go to bed?

JAN. Fine! Now, gimme'!

*(**MITCHELL** hands her the diary and the two exit through the SL door.*

*After a brief pause, **PAWPAW** enters through the Kitchen door.)*

PAWPAW. Will you turn down that music? *(He starts idly snapping his fingers.)* What is that, anyway? Who's playing that? *(He moves to the entertainment center and looks it.)* How does this thing work? *(He doesn't touch anything.)* That's the kind of stuff we used to listen to.

*(At this moment, a Big Band tune begins playing, softly at first. The slow dance tune gets louder as **PAWPAW** turns toward the front door. It slowly opens at the same time the area around the front door becomes bathed in a blue spot as if illuminated by moonlight. Then **LORI**, wearing a dress from the 1950's, dances into the room. She stops and looks at **PAWPAW**. She puts out her arms.)*

LORI. Do you hear it? It's our song, Bear.

PAWPAW. Lori?

LORI. We so loved this song, don't you remember?

PAWPAW. But… you…

LORI. Dance with me, Bear. You still know how to dance. Remember, when I taught you?

(PAWPAW moves to her as if in a dream.)

PAWPAW. You are so pretty. You were always the prettiest one in the room.

LORI. Oh, you'll never change.

PAWPAW. Nor will you.

LORI. Dance with me, Bear.

(The two embrace and slowly dance to the music.)

PAWPAW. You were always SO smooth. So light on your feet.

LORI. You remember the first time we heard this song?

PAWPAW. Of course. Well,… no.

LORI. It was our favorite. We used to dance to them all.

PAWPAW. We did. I… miss that.

LORI. And I'd save all the slow dances for you.

PAWPAW. Lori, listen to me! *(He stops and she looks at him.)* I think of you every day, I miss you every day, why – ?

LORI. No one could dance like you, Bear. Dance with me, Bear.

PAWPAW. I… I will. Any time. You just… *(LORI waltzes slowly out the door.)* Lori? No, Don't go! Lori! *(He moves to the door and yells.)* LORI! DON'T GO! LORI?! *(He bolts out the door as the LIGHTS change back to their original hues.)*

(AUSTIN enters through the SL door, dressed in his robe.)

AUSTIN. Pawpaw! What? *(He looks around.)*

(MARY JO, also in her robe, enters behind him)

MARY JO. What's going on? Where's Dad?

PAWPAW. *(Offstage.)* LORI! COME BACK! DON'T GO! PLEASE!

AUSTIN. He's outside again!

(There is the sound of a car screeching to a stop and it's horn blaring.)

MARY JO. DAD!

AUSTIN. PAWPAW! *(He rushes out the door and **MARY JO** stops at the doorway and looks out.)*

MARY JO. DAD! DAD!

*(**MITCHELL** and **JAN** enter quickly through the SL door and wait nervously as the LIGHTS dim out and end the ACT.)*

ACT II

Scene one

"Don't answer the door"

*(It is now two weeks later. **JAN** is standing, looking out the window. Then, as if she sees something, she quickly sits in the recliner and picks up a magazine. Realizing after a bit that it's upside down, the turns it over just as **MARY JO** and **AUSTIN** enter through the kitchen door. **MARY JO** has obviously been crying as she dabs her eyes with a crumpled tissue.)*

MARY JO. *(As they enter.)* ...I know what he said but he could be wrong, you know?

AUSTIN. He's consulted with other doctors, hon.

JAN. *(Leans up.)* How's Pawpaw?

AUSTIN. About the same, he's... uh he's still in bed, of course.

JAN. *(Gets up.)* Still? Shouldn't he be back walking again?

MARY JO. These things take time, hon, he got pretty banged up, remember.

JAN. But when's he coming home?

MARY JO. We don't know.

JAN. Dumb doctors! *(She exits out the SL door.)*

MARY JO. She's right about that. *(**AUSTIN** looks at her.)* Dumb doctors! *(She sits on the couch and again dabs her eyes.)*

*(**AUSTIN** pulls out a brochure from his inside jacket pocket and looks at it. He then looks at **MARY JO**.)*

AUSTIN. *(Moves to her.)* Will you, at least, look at this?

MARY JO. I'm not putting him in one of those places.

AUSTIN. Mary Jo, we cannot watch him twenty-four hours a day. *(He points to the front door.)* And next time he might not be so lucky –

MARY JO. I know, I know!

AUSTIN. *(Hands the brochure to her.)* Will you read this? That's all, just read it.

MARY JO. Fine. *(She takes the brochure.)*

AUSTIN. He's going to be in the hospital for another week anyway. Then –

MARY JO. We'll cross that bridge when we come to it. *(She looks up at* **AUSTIN***, who takes her hand, and smiles.)* Another old saying, shame Jan missed it.

AUSTIN. *(Trying to lighten the mood.)* Yep, we got a million of 'em. *(He stretches and yawns.)* Is there anything to eat?

MARY JO. Oh! You and Dale! That's all you ever think about.

AUSTIN. Speaking of which, have you heard from those two – from those lovely sisters of yours?

MARY JO. I saw Val at the hospital two days ago but it's been over a week since I've heard ANYthing out of Brenda.

AUSTIN. *(Moving to the kitchen door.)* Well, at least that's ONE good thing that's come out of all this.

MARY JO. *(Looks back.)* I thought you LIKED Brenda?

AUSTIN. Oh! I DO! A real sweetheart. Salt of the earth! She's in my will! Are you buying any of this?

MARY JO. Just go eat.

AUSTIN. I'm'a goin'. *(He exits into the kitchen.)*

*(***MARY JO*** looks through the brochure. After a bit, the phone rings.* ***MARY JO*** *gets up and moves to the desk, where she picks up the receiver.)*

MARY JO. Hello? Jan, I got it. Thank you. Hello? Brenda! We were just talking about you, where have you – ? No, we just got back from the hospital. What? He'll be there for at least another week. No, probably longer. You did WHAT?! But… But… But… When… But… Why… But… But… Who… But… Well, sure, you can, but… But… *(***JAN*** enters through the SL door, eating a sandwich.*

She moves to her mother.) But… Fine. No, no problem. But… Okay. Bye. *(She hangs up the phone and looks at* **JAN**.*)* Where did you get that sandwich?

JAN. I always keep one in my room for special occasions.

MARY JO. Listen, will you go into Pawpaw's room and change the sheets.

JAN. Me? Why do I always have to do all the work around here?

MARY JO. Let me rephrase that; you seem to think this is a discussion. GO into Pawpaw's room and CHANGE the sheets.

JAN. OHP! *(She stamps her feet and stomps out of the room, exiting out the SL door.)*

*(***AUSTIN** *looks out the kitchen door.)*

AUSTIN. Who ate all the bologna?

MARY JO. Did you look everywhere? In the 'fridgerator?

AUSTIN. I did.

MARY JO. Did you check Jan's room?

AUSTIN. What?

MARY JO. *(Moves to* **AUSTIN**.*)* Dear? Sweetheart? Darling?

AUSTIN. And no, I'm not buying any of that. What did you do now?

MARY JO. *(Taking* **AUSTIN***'s hand.)* We need to have a little talk. *(She leads him over to the couch and seats the suspicious husband.)*

AUSTIN. You're not going to propose, are you?

MARY JO. *(Sits next to him.)* It's been done. Listen, hon, we're a family, right?

AUSTIN. Oh, geez, it's relatives!

MARY JO. This is important; let me finish.

AUSTIN. Oh, geez, it's YOUR relatives.

MARY JO. You were asking about Brenda a second ago, right?

AUSTIN. *(Moves away slightly.)* Yeees?

MARY JO. That was her, on the phone.

AUSTIN. Aaannnd?

MARY JO. She needs a favor.

AUSTIN. Oh, great! How much does she want THIS time?

MARY JO. Will you let me finish?

AUSTIN. Just tell me how much?

MARY JO. WILL you let me finish?!

AUSTIN. Just give me a ballpark figure so I'll know how many parts of my body to clench.

MARY JO. It's not money.

AUSTIN. *(Unbelieving.)* It's not.

MARY JO. No.

AUSTIN. Are you sure it was Brenda? *(MARY JO looks away, now a bit miffed, and crosses her arms.)* OKAY. I'm SORRY. What does Brenda want?

(JAN looks in through the SL door. AUSTIN and MARY JO look at her.)

JAN. Mom, what sheets do you want me to put on Pawpaw's bed?

(Slowly, AUSTIN turns back to MARY JO.)

AUSTIN. *(Deeply felt.)* Ooohhh, noooo!

JAN. She and Dale had a fight –

(AUSTIN jumps to his feet.)

AUSTIN. Again?! So what's new about that?

MARY JO. Well, this one was different.

AUSTIN. Than the seventy-three others?

JAN. Are you two going to get into some big thing now?

MARY JO. No!

AUSTIN. Yes!

JAN. *(Casually)* I'll… I'll just go find some sheets, don't worry about – *(She points to herself and quickly exits.)*

AUSTIN. And now she wants to ambush us?

MARY JO. *(Calmly.)* One person does not an ambush make.

AUSTIN. Yeah? Have you been in front of her when she's talking? It's like Surround-Sound. *(He quickly moves to the desk.)*

(**MARY JO** *leaps to her feet and follows* **AUSTIN** *over to the desk.*)

MARY JO. She left him and now she needs a place to stay.

AUSTIN. She should've thought about that before she left him.

MARY JO. She just wants to stay here until it blows over.

AUSTIN. And what did you tell her? (**MARY JO** *starts to speak but then looks at the floor.*) That's what I thought. (*He picks up the receiver.*) You call her right back and tell her she can't stay here.

MARY JO. I can't tell her that.

AUSTIN. You tell her something. Tell her you have to talk it over with me, SOMEthing!

MARY JO. She's not at home; she called on her cell phone.

AUSTIN. I don't care. (*He holds out the receiver.*) Tell her.

MARY JO. Fine! (*She dials a number and puts the receiver to her ear.*)

(*Offstage, just outside the front door, a cell phone rings.* **AUSTIN** *hears this and looks around. Slowly, he turns to look at the door as it rings again.*)

BRENDA. (*In muffled tones.*) Hello?

MARY JO. Brenda? Me.

BRENDA. So, what did he say?

MARY JO. He says we need to talk it over.

(**AUSTIN** *moves to the front door.*)

BRENDA. What's the big deal? I thought he liked me. And here, the one time I ask a favor, he turns out to be some sort of – (**AUSTIN** *opens the door to find* **BRENDA**, *standing between a large suitcase and a pet carry-all case and talking into her cell phone*) – overbearing jerk tyrant! (*She turns to see* **AUSTIN**. *She smiles.*) Hell-Ooo. (*She points to her phone.*) We were just talking about you. (*She picks up the carry-all case*). Say hello, Charlemaine. (*From inside the case a fierce yapping is heard.*)

(*LIGHTS black out.*)

Scene Two

(It is now three days later, in the afternoon. **TISH** *is sitting on the couch, while* **MITCHELL** *stands nearby.)*

TISH. I still think you're dropping a lot on your family at one time.

MITCHELL. Now, hon, I think I know them pretty well. You just let me worry about them.

TISH. Maybe if we let them in on the decision.

MITCHELL. Here's an idea; I thought about this last night. You handle your family and I'll handle mine. *(She looks at him curiously and he sits on the couch arm.)* I mean once we're married I'll deal with my group, how to tell them things and when, and you can do the same for yours.

TISH. I guess that seems about right. I just have a bad feeling about coming over here today?

MITCHELL. *(Moves to the SL door.)* Why? What makes you think that?

*(***MITCHELL*** opens the SL door and* **MARY JO** *and* **BRENDA** *can be heard arguing.)*

BRENDA. *(Offstage.)* Don't tell ME about being married!
MARY JO. *(Offstage.)* I'm not trying to tell you anything!
BRENDA. You are so!
MARY JO. I am NOT!

*(***MITCHELL*** shuts the door and looks at* **TISH.**)*

MITCHELL. *(After a slight pause.)* Mom'll be right out.

(Just then **JAN** *enters quickly through the SL door and, shutting it, leans against it.)*

JAN. Hey, Mitch! How'd you like to take Aunt Brenda home with you?

MITCHELL. *(Trying to change the subject.)* Hi, Jan.

JAN. I'll give you eight dollars. *(She elbows him slightly.)* But there's more in it for you as soon as I get my allowance.

MITCHELL. Let me see what I can do. *(He exits out the door.)*

(JAN turns to TISH and stares at her. There is an uneasy silence between the two.)

TISH. Hi.

JAN. Hi.

TISH. *(After another pause.)* So.

JAN. Yeah.

TISH. *(After another pause.)* Okay,

JAN. Whatever.

TISH. Why don't you like me?

JAN. *(Softening.)* No, it's not I don't like you – Gah.

TISH. I know. We sprung all this on everyone all at once. And you miss how things used to be.

JAN. *(Amazed.)* Yeah. *(She moves to TISH.)* How'd you know?

TISH. Well, when I was – *(She pats the couch seat next to her and JAN sits)* – when I was your age I went through stuff, too.

JAN. Like what kinda' stuff?

TISH. You know my real mother died when I was a kid and when I was about your age my Dad told me he was going to marry someone else.

JAN. Wow. Did you know her?

TISH. Yeah, they'd been seeing each other for some time. But when he told me he wanted to marry her, I'm sorry; I just didn't like her at all.

JAN. But it wasn't her, was it? I mean, it wasn't REALLY her.

TISH. That's right. It was just that everything seemed to be changing too fast, seemed to be –

JAN. Out of control. *(She looks out.)* First, you guys and your big announcement and then Pawpaw… *(She looks off.)*

TISH. *(She leans in to JAN.)* I like her now, though. Took awhile but I do.

JAN. *(Looks at TISH, not sure.)* Okay, I'll give you a chance. But you gotta' do me a favor.

TISH. What?

JAN. Will you take Aunt Brenda home with you? *(*TISH *laughs.)* I promise, I'll NEVER ask for anything else!

*(*MARY JO *and* MITCHELL *enter through the SL door.)*

MARY JO. Tish, I'm sorry to make you wait out here with our little hoodlum there.

TISH. Oh, she's not too bad. We were just having a talk, us girls.

JAN. Yes, we were.

MARY JO. Well, I'd like to tell you this is unusual for our family but –

MITCHELL. It's not.

TISH. Mitch told me about Aunt Brenda and Uncle Dale.

MITCHELL. *(Nudges* MARY JO.*)* 'Aunt Brenda and Uncle Dale,' I love it when she talks like that.

MARY JO. Now, what is it you two want to drop on us today?

MITCHELL. *(Mock surprise.)* Oh, Mom! You're SO suspicious. *(She turns to him.)* It's nothing! Really. We just set the date, that's all.

JAN. What?

TISH. Hey!

MITCHELL. What?

TISH. I was going to tell Jan before anyone else.

JAN. You were?

TISH. *(Looks at* JAN.*)* Of course. And after that I was going to ask you to be a 'Lady in Waiting'.

JAN. Ooooh! *(She stands up and walks around, with one hand, hanging limply at the wrist, out in front of her.)* A Lady in Waiting. Me. Well, fiddle-dee- dee. *(She stops and turns to* TISH.*)* I'm not going to have to wear one of those turquoise and orange chiffon things, am I?

TISH. Of course not.

JAN. Good!

MITCHELL. No, we were thinking turquoise and purple. *(He looks at* MARY JO.*)* School colors. *(He notices* MARY JO *is* *still staring at him. He tries to laugh it off.)* I'm kidding! *(He drops the smile.)* What?

MARY JO. Set the date?

MITCHELL. OH! I guess we ran past that pretty good, huh?

MARY JO. I guess you did.

(**AUSTIN**, *wearing a business suit and carrying a briefcase, enters through the kitchen door.)*

AUSTIN. I'm home, boys and girls. Oh, hi, Tish! *(He moves to* **MARY JO**.*)* And how was your day, dear? *(He kisses her on the cheek and then notices the look on her face.)* What? What'd I do now?

MARY JO. It's not you; why do you always think it's you?

AUSTIN. Usually saves time.

MARY JO. Mitchell just told me they have set the date for the wedding. *(To* **MITCHELL**.*)* Wedding?

MITCHELL. Uh, no. *(He moves to* **TISH**.*)* We set the date for the reception. But we figure to have the wedding sometime before that.

JAN. And I get to be a Lady in Waiting.

AUSTIN. *(Moves to the couch.)* Well, congratulations, you two. When is it?

MARY JO. We were just getting to that.

(**BRENDA**, *now dressed in a house robe, enters through the SL door. She is eating a sandwich.)*

BRENDA. *(Through chews.)* I thought I heard Austin's car.

MARY JO. *(Wheels on* **BRENDA**.*)* We're just about to have dinner, Brenda, can't you wait.

BRENDA. *(Caught off guard.)* You didn't say anything.

MARY JO. Where'd you get that sandwich?

BRENDA. Jan's room.

JAN. *(Appalled.)* WHAT?!

BRENDA. Have you been in there; that place is stocked.

(**JAN** *rushes over to* **BRENDA**.*)*

JAN. Aunt Brenda, that's MY room! You can't just go in there and take whatever you want, I don't care if –

AUSTIN. Jan!

JAN. What?!

AUSTIN. *(Points at her.)* Take it down a couple of notches!

JAN. But –

MARY JO. Just go to your room and find something to keep yourself busy.

JAN. Fine! *(She moves to the SL door.)* I see how it works now. Everybody gets to do what THEY want, it doesn't matter what I want!

AUSTIN. Quietly?

JAN. As long as I do it quietly. Oh, I know. I'll clean up my room. *(She leans in to the group.)* You never know when company's going to drop in!

MARY JO. Jan?! *(She points to the door.)*

JAN. Ohp! *(She stamps her foot and exits.)*

AUSTIN. *(Smiling.)* And there it is, the patented Jan Rogers One-Step. *(He imitates* **JAN.***)* Ohp! *(He stamps his foot.)*

BRENDA. She has such a mouth on her.

*(***MARY JO*** turns to her.)*

MITCHELL. *(Trying to continue)* Anyway, we wanted you two to be the first to know. *(***TISH*** nudges him.)* Uh, second to know. *(He smiles sheepishly.)*

TISH. *(Leans forward.)* We already told my folks.

AUSTIN. How'd they take it?

TISH. About like I thought they would – Dad's still giggling and Mom's still crying.

AUSTIN. Wait'll he gets the bill for the wedding. He'll stop giggling.

MARY JO. So. *(She sits on the couch next to* **TISH.***)* When IS the date?

TISH. November seventeenth. That's the one-year anniversary from when we met.

MARY JO. Is it too late to say I think you're rushing into this?

*(***MITCHELL*** looks at his watch.)*

MITCHELL. It is... right... *(He brings a hand down)*... now!

BRENDA. Oh, for heaven's sake, you and Austin were younger than they are when you got married.

MARY JO. Brenda? Do you mind? This is family.

BRENDA. And what am I? *(AUSTIN starts to speak but BRENDA points at him.)* I asked Mary Jo.

TISH. We talked this over and we thought – *(She looks at MITCHELL.)*

MITCHELL. We thought it would give everyone time for any objections, for any arrangements, for anything to get settled. It's still six months away, you know.

MARY JO. I know! *(She rises.)*

AUSTIN. Very nice of you both to consider us, isn't it, Mary Jo.

MARY JO. I said I know!

BRENDA. More than you gave Dad and Mom, I remember that.

MARY JO. You want to stop helping now?

(JAN looks in through the SL door.)

JAN. Aunt Brenda, your dog just ran out the back door.

BRENDA. *(Appalled.)* What? *(She rushes to the door.)* How'd that happen?

JAN. *(Mock surprise.)* I don't know. *(She shrugs.)*

(BRENDA exits quickly as JAN moves to AUSTIN.)

AUSTIN. *(To JAN.)* Good one! *(He tries to keep from laughing.)* That thing is such a fitful, yelping –

JAN. How much longer is she going to be here, Mom?

AUSTIN. Jan, it's not all that bad; she's only been here a week.

(MARY JO takes a long pause as she slowly turns to AUSTIN.)

MARY JO. She's been here three days.

AUSTIN & JAN. You're kidding!

MARY JO. Can we stick to one subject here?

MITCHELL. Fine. Now. *(He moves* **MARY JO** *back to the couch and seats her.)* That's why we're here so we can talk this out.

AUSTIN. Another good idea. *(***MARY JO** *looks at him.)* I'll shut up now.

MARY JO. No! You're going to put your two-cents into this as well.

AUSTIN. Okay, here it is. *(He sits on the couch arm.)* I say this. You can talk about marriage, you can read about marriage, you can see videos and listen to tapes about marriage. You can talk with other people who are married. You can dream about marriage or have nightmares about marriage. You can rush into marriage, you can make up a list, citing pros and cons about marriage. You can research it, analyze it, dissect it, run a history on it and make jokes about it. But nobody, and I mean NO-BODY, can prepare you for what marriage really is until you actually, physically, get married.

MARY JO. How long have you been working on that?

AUSTIN. How long have we been married? *(He quickly smiles.)* I'm kidding, I know how long we've been married. *(He leans into* **MARY JO.***)* And you recall how it was when we first got married?

MARY JO. *(Remembering.)* I was just thinking of that. We, too, were very much in love.

AUSTIN. And still are.

MARY JO. *(Leans against* **AUSTIN.***)* I was coming to that. *(She looks at* **TISH.***)* And still are.

JAN. Oh, GROSS! *(She exits through the kitchen door.)*

AUSTIN. Then there's the downside. *(He leans in to* **TISH.***)* You may have children.

MITCHELL. We're prepared for that. I figure they'll be like me. *(He poses dramatically.)*

AUSTIN. They could be like your Aunt Brenda.

(Everyone looks at each other and all, except **TISH,** *shudder.)*

MARY JO. That's not very nice!

AUSTIN. You shuddered, too!

MARY JO. But it still wouldn't hurt to talk about it first.

MITCHELL. And that's what we want to do.

(The doorbell sounds.)

AUSTIN. Now what? *(He moves to the front door.)*

MARY JO. Get rid of them; I don't want anything to interrupt us now.

AUSTIN. Of course. **(AUSTIN** *opens the door to find* **DALE.)** Dale! *(He pulls* **DALE** *into the room.)* I am SO glad you're here!

MARY JO. Dale? *(She rises.)*

AUSTIN. Brenda's just dying to come home; she forgives you for everything. And even if she doesn't, I'll help you tie her up.

MARY JO. Dale, this isn't a good time; we're just having a very serious talk with Mitchell and… *(She points to* **TISH** *but cannot recall her name.)*

TISH. *(After a pause.)* Tish.

MARY JO. Right. *(She tries to laugh it off.)* Sorry, dear.

DALE. Uhm… where IS Brenda?

AUSTIN. I'll get her! *(He sprints to the SL door.)* You just wait right here; I won't be a moment! *(He opens the SL door and a loud yapping is heard. He looks back at* **DALE.)** And don't forget little Charlemaine. *(He yells out the door.)* Brenda!

DALE. I am SO sorry you've had to put up with all this. Hi, Mitch.

MITCHELL. Uncle Dale.

DALE. Listen, guys, I need a favor.

MARY JO. What?

AUSTIN. How much? *(He whips out a checkbook from his inside coat pocket.)* You just say the amount and take Brenda and I'll write you a check so fast!

*(***BRENDA** *enters through the SL door.)*

BRENDA. Well, little Charlemaine is back now but so full of weeds I'll need the bathroom for at least 3 hours. *(She sees* **DALE.***)* Oh. *(She turns away and folds her arms.)* It's you.

DALE. *(Moves to* **BRENDA.***)* Yes, Brenda, it's me. Who did you think it was?

BRENDA. Come to apologize?

AUSTIN. *(Grinning.)* Yes, he has! *(He drops the smile and turns to* **DALE.***)* You have, right?

DALE. I did not.

AUSTIN. Oh, great. *(He looks at* **TISH.***)* You can watch marriage, you can listen to marriage –

BRENDA. Then why DID you come here?

DALE. Well – *(He sheepishly looks at the others and then back at* **BRENDA.***)* Just have something I think you ought to know.

BRENDA. And that is?

DALE. *(Clumsily.)* Last night... the thing is, well,...

BRENDA. Well, what?

DALE. There... there was a fire.

BRENDA. *(Turns to* **DALE.***)* A fire? In our neighborhood?

DALE. Yes.

BRENDA. On our block?

DALE. Yes.

*(***BRENDA*** stares at him for a long pause.)*

MITCHELL. I think it's this next question, which will be the important one.

BRENDA. Our ho... our hou... our... *(She swallows hard)*... it was our hou... se?

DALE. *(Nods.)* The fire department is still investigating it.

(Now numb, **BRENDA** *stares out.)*

MARY JO. Oh dear!

DALE. *(Turns to the others.)* So, I hope it will be all right... I mean, if I can stay with you for awhile, too. *(He turns* *to* **BRENDA**.*)* I can stay in the same room with Brenda, right, cupcake? *(He puts an arm around* **BRENDA**, *who scowls at him.)*

AUSTIN. *(Voice cracking.)* Mitchell, I think we'll put off that little talk for now.

(LIGHTS dim out.)

Scene Three

*(It is two days later. **VAL** is sitting on the couch, talking with **JAN**.)*

JAN. *(Giving **VAL** the dish.)* THEN Aunt Brenda starts in about Uncle Dale, how he's such a slob and always sneaks around smoking cigars and staying out late and, you know –

VAL. Being a man.

JAN. Uh huh. But Mom keeps telling her that she needs to take a look at herself, that she's no prize, that she has things that he has to put up with and isn't all that easy to live with, either.

VAL. Which she denies.

JAN. Uh huh. Then Dad tries to point out what she and Dale have in common and both Mom and Aunt Brenda turn on him –

VAL. And tell him to shut up?

JAN. Uh huh. Was Aunt Brenda ALWAYS like this?

VAL. Right down to her over-pedicured toes. NObody has problems like she has, to hear her tell it. Now. *(She leans in to **JAN**.)* You want to hear problems, let me tell you about MY life.

JAN. *(Yells.)* Mom?! Aunt Val is waiting!

*(The SL door open and **MARY JO** enters.)*

MARY JO. Sorry, Val, I was talking with your hard-headed sister!

VAL. How bad is it?

*(Offstage we hear **DALE** and **BRENDA** arguing.)*

BRENDA. Stop picking at my shoulder! That's a beauty mark!

DALE. That is NOT a beauty mark!

BRENDA. That's a beauty mark!

DALE. Beauty marks don't drain!

*(**MARY JO** closes the door.)*

MARY JO. I'll just get my purse and then we can go see Dad. *(She moves to the desk.)*

VAL. *(Rises.)* Mary Jo, you really shouldn't have to do everything. *(She moves to MARY JO.)* You're always the one going to see Dad and on top of that having to put up with Brenda and her lapdog.

JAN. That Charlemaine really IS a pain.

VAL. *(To JAN.)* I wasn't talking about Charlemaine. *(She looks at MARY JO for a beat, then the two burst out laughing.)*

MARY JO. Oh, thank you! I needed a good laugh.

VAL. Good. I'm glad I could do SOMEthing to help. You know I'd take Dale and Brenda but –

MARY JO. You only have that small apartment, I know.

(AUSTIN enters through the kitchen door.)

VAL. Listen, why don't you take a night off.

MARY JO. What?

AUSTIN. Now, THAT's the best idea I've heard yet.

MARY JO. What do you mean, take a night off?

VAL. I'll go see Dad.

AUSTIN. That's VERY nice of you, Val.

MARY JO. I don't know…

VAL. I'm a big girl now, I know the way. *(She leans over to catch MARY JO's gaze.)* I can drive and everything.

(MARY JO again smiles and looks at AUSTIN.)

AUSTIN. We'll go out to dinner, maybe take in a movie, it'll be like a date.

MARY JO. But I really have a bad feeling about this. What about Brenda?

(JAN jumps up and moves to her mother.)

JAN. Hey, they're going to fight whether you're here or not.

VAL. Right. And Jan here can tell you everything you missed.

JAN. Yeah!

VAL. She's told me everything that's gone on over here; she can do the same for you.

MARY JO. Jan!

JAN. Well? Aunt Val asked! And you don't want me to lie, do you?

VAL. No, dear, we don't want you to lie. *(She leans in to* **JAN**.*)* I didn't tell you about me and Mr. Carter, did I?

JAN. No!

MARY JO. What about you and Bill Carter?

VAL. Never mind! *(She ushers* **MARY JO** *to the front door.)* You two go out and have a good time. *(***AUSTIN**, *now smiling, follows.)*

MARY JO. Okay! Jan, you tell Brenda where we went.

JAN. If I find an opening.

AUSTIN. Thank you, Val. I've been trying to get Mary Jo out of this house for days now.

VAL. Then go!

(Just then the front door opens and **MITCHELL** *enters.)*

MITCHELL. Oh! Hey, everyone. What's going on?

MARY JO. Nothing, dear. Is there anything wrong?

MITCHELL. Well –

VAL. If there is, WE can handle it! *(She stares at* **MITCHELL**.*)* Right, Mitchell?

MITCHELL. Uhh,… sure!

VAL. See? So you two are free to just forget about everything and enjoy your evening out.

AUSTIN. And we will. I'll take it from here.

MARY JO. Hold it! *(She stops at the door.)*

VAL. What?

MARY JO. This won't work.

VAL. Don't give me any excuses.

MARY JO. I have to. We can't leave this way!

VAL. And why not?!

AUSTIN. *(Leans in to* **VAL**.*)* The garage is through the kitchen.

VAL. Oh, for heaven's sake! *(She ushers MARY JO over to the kitchen door.)* Get out! And I mean now!

(MARY JO starts to say something but AUSTIN opens the door. She smiles at him and they both exit.)

JAN. I've tried to raise them right but, you know, a teenager can only do so much.

(VAL turns to MITCHELL.)

VAL. We figured your Mom could use some time off.

MITCHELL. I guess. *(He looks down.)* I probably shouldn't have come over here tonight.

VAL. What now? I thought you all had sat down, discussed the wedding and gotten all the objections out of the way?

MITCHELL. Not yet we haven't.

VAL. Don't TELL me Mary Jo is still against it.

MITCHELL. Well, it doesn't matter much, either way. *(He looks at VAL.)* We broke up.

(VAL and JAN look at each other. VAL takes MITCHELL's hand and leads him to the couch.)

VAL. *(Resigned to helping.)* What happened? *(She sits.)*

MITCHELL. Great. NOW somebody wants to talk about it.

(MITCHELL moves to the couch as the LIGHTS black out.)

Scene Four

(It is later that night. **AUSTIN** *enters from the kitchen and throws the car keys on the desk. He is obviously not in a good mood.* **MARY JO** *enters behind him and moves to the SL door.)*

AUSTIN. *(Trying to hold his temper.)* All I said was you shouldn't think you have to take on the whole world and solve everybody's problems.

MARY JO. *(Stops and turns.)* That's not what you said. You said I was poking my nose in where it didn't belong.

AUSTIN. No, I did not! Some night out!

MARY JO. She is my sister and if I can't help her –

AUSTIN. NObody can help her!

MARY JO. She's family! People help each other in a family!

AUSTIN. Yeah, to the point where they can't help themselves?!

MARY JO. Just… don't talk to me! *(She exits out the SL door and slams it.)*

AUSTIN. *(Muttering to himself.)* Where did I… ? *(He motions with his hands as if he's seating someone.)* At dinner… *(He indicates himself)* …she had the veal, I had steak. *(He indicates another person.)* She said… *(He mouths something)* …and I said *(He again mouths something).* And by the time we had dessert… *(He puts his hands on his hips and mouths something in a much fiercer manner. He stops and thinks.)* Oh, yeah! *(He crosses to the SL door and opens it. A pillow and blanket comes flying into his arms.)* I'm supposed to sleep out here?

MARY JO. *(Looks in.)* You figure it out! Remember, I can't stick my nose where it doesn't belong! *(She pulls the door shut.)*

*(***AUSTIN*** throws the pillow and blanket on the recliner.)*

AUSTIN. I don't believe this! You say one wrong thing and end up on the couch! *(He begins taking the cushions off the couch and pulling out the hide-a-bed. About halfway* *through,* **DALE**, *wearing a robe, enters quietly through the SL door and begins helping* **AUSTIN**. **AUSTIN** *looks up at* **DALE**.*)* What're you doing?

DALE. Helping you make up our bed.

AUSTIN. *(Straightens up.)* Well, thank – OUR bed? Since when do YOU have to sleep out here?

DALE. Since a few minutes ago when Brenda found out from Mary Jo that you have a hide-a-bed in the couch.

AUSTIN. Oh, Geez! I don't believe ANY of this!

DALE. *(Sees sheets on the bed.)* You always keep sheets on the hide-a-bed? (**AUSTIN** *gives him a disgusted look.*) Oh. Been here, done that.

AUSTIN. This is all your fault, you know! (He throws the pillow and blanket on the bed.

DALE. Hey, don't jump on me. I'm one of the few people still talking to you.

AUSTIN. Well, there's too much talk in this family, if you ask me! *(He starts taking off his shirt, revealing his T-shirt.)*

DALE. I know what you mean. *(He pulls off his robe to reveal some very loud pajamas.)*

AUSTIN. I don't know why we just can't let people alone, you know? I try and try to tell Mary Jo – *(He turns to see* **DALE.***)* What, in GOD's name, are you wearing?

DALE. Pajamas; what do you sleep in?

AUSTIN. *(Sits on the bed.)* Let me see if I understand this. Your house is on fire, you know you could possibly lose everything you own… and you grab THOSE?!

DALE. These aren't mine!

AUSTIN. Where did you get them?

DALE. From your wife!

AUSTIN. Where did SHE get them?

DALE. Well, put it this way. *(He sings.)* 'Happy Birthday to you, happy birthday to you…' *(He poses.)* Well? What do you think?

AUSTIN. They make your butt look big; will you just shut up and go to bed!

DALE. Sor-RY!

(AUSTIN sits on the side of the bed and begins taking off his shoes.)

AUSTIN. This is really getting out of hand.

DALE. Uhm… why are you sitting there?

AUSTIN. *(Trying to be patient.)* I have to sit somewhere to take off my shoes

DALE. Yeah, but –

AUSTIN. Yeah, but WHAT?

DALE. I sleep on that side of the bed.

AUSTIN. Listen, Felix, you're in MY house – I sleep on whichever side I want to sleep on!

DALE. FINE! *(He throws himself into the bed.)*

AUSTIN. GREAT! *(He takes off his pants to reveal a very loud pair of boxer shorts. DALE sits up and stares at the shorts. AUSTIN puts his pants on the recliner and turns to see DALE staring at his shorts. He looks at them and back at DALE.)* Christmas present.

DALE. Yeah.

AUSTIN. I was going to surprise Mary Jo when we got back and went to bed, I thought she'd – why am I telling you ALL THIS?!

DALE. *(Calmly.)* I have no idea.

(AUSTIN gets in bed next to DALE and put the pillow under his head. The two lie quietly for a brief pause.)

DALE. How come you get the pillow?

AUSTIN. You want to hear the house rules again; shut up!

DALE. I can't sleep without a pillow!

AUSTIN. *(Leans over to DALE.)* They have LOTS of pillows in a motel!

DALE. I just asked!

AUSTIN. Fine! *(He lies down again.)*

(DALE grabs his robe, bundles it up and uses it for a pillow.)

(Another brief pause.)

DALE. Also, I snore.

(AUSTIN sits up suddenly and then turns to DALE.)

AUSTIN. You wake me up ONCE, just ONCE, with your snoring and I'll take MY pillow and smother you in your SLEEP!

DALE. *(Sits up.)* Look, I don't like this any more than you do!

AUSTIN. Yeah? You know what you can do, don't you?!

DALE. Yes, I do! *(He gets up.)* I'll go sleep in the car!

AUSTIN. *(Also gets to his feet.)* Fine! But not MY car! *(He crosses to DALE.)* If you hadn't been smoking those cheap cigars your house probably wouldn't have burned down!

DALE. That was NOT what started the fire!

(BRENDA enters through the SL door.)

AUSTIN. I'm just saying what Brenda told me!

DALE. You're going to believer HER?!

BRENDA. What's THAT supposed to mean?

AUSTIN. He means – *(Realizing suddenly he is in his shorts, he quickly looks around and grabs DALE's robe and puts it on.)* Nothing!

DALE. I didn't think you were talking to me?

(The phone rings. AUSTIN stomps over to the desk.)

BRENDA. I WASN'T talking to you! I was talking to him!

DALE. And making up stories, just to make sure they're on YOUR side?

AUSTIN. *(Into the receiver.)* Hello?! *(Quieter.)* I mean, yes?

BRENDA. They're my family.

DALE. I'm part of this family, too.

AUSTIN. Dr. Parnell? What?

BRENDA. And don't tell me I'm making up ANYthing! *(AUSTIN waves her to quieten down.)* What? Don't YOU start telling me what to do!

AUSTIN. *(Receiver to his chest.)* Get Mary Jo!

BRENDA. What?

AUSTIN. Hurry!

(MARY JO enters through the SL door.)

MARY JO. Will you people PLEASE stop yelling?!

AUSTIN. *(Tentatively.)* Hon? It's Dr. Parnell.

MARY JO. Oh my – *(She rushes over to the phone.* **BRENDA** *follows her over.)*

AUSTIN. It's Pawpaw. He… he…

MARY JO. *(Fearful.)* Oh no! *(***AUSTIN** *nods his head slowly and looks at* **DALE***, who looks down.* **BRENDA** *clutches a robe sleeve to her mouth.* **MARY JO** *gently takes the receiver.)*

MARY JO. *(Into the receiver.)* Dr. Parnell? What… what happened?

(LIGHTS dim out.)

ACT III

"A photo finish"

(It is three days later, in the late afternoon. The room is lit only by the setting sun through the front window. **MARY JO**, *now wearing mourning, as is everyone else in the family, looks out through the drapes. There are half empty glasses and plates around the room as if company had just left.* **JAN**, *also dressed in mourning, sits on the couch.* **VAL** *enters through the kitchen and picks up a pair of glasses from the sofa table. She looks at* **MARY JO**.*)*

VAL. It's getting dark?

MARY JO. *(Absently.)* What?

VAL. *(Indicates the room.)* It's getting dark in here.

MARY JO. Oh, I guess it is. *(She turns on two switches near the front door. The first switch illuminates the area near the door and the second switch lights the rest of the area.)*
(**AUSTIN** *enters from the kitchen and looks at* **MARY JO**. **VAL** *moves to the door, nudges* **AUSTIN** *and nods toward* **MARY JO**. *He nods back and* **VAL** *exits out the door.* **AUSTIN** *crosses to* **MARY JO**, *who is again at the window. He gently puts his hands on her shoulders.)*

AUSTIN. You didn't eat anything.

MARY JO. Not hungry.

AUSTIN. Hon, I know you're angry at me – *(She looks at his curiously)* – I wish I could change it, you know that. We SHOULD'VE gone to see him that last night.

MARY JO. Wouldn't have helped.

AUSTIN. I can see it's eating at you.

MARY JO. *(Evenly.)* I'm all right.

AUSTIN. I spoke with Dr. Parnell, did I tell you?

MARY JO. Can you do something – ? *(She indicates* **JAN.***)*

AUSTIN. *(Also looks at* **JAN.***)* Oh. I'll try.

MARY JO. *(Looking around.)* This place is a mess. *(She picks up two plates from the desk and exits out the kitchen door.)*

AUSTIN. *(Moving over to* **JAN.***)* How're you doing, pun'kin?

JAN. Pun'kin? You haven't called me that in –

AUSTIN. *(Sitting next to her.)* Quite a while, I know. Too long. *(He puts an arm around* **JAN,** *who leans in to him.)*

JAN. Pawpaw called me that.

AUSTIN. Yeah. He had names for all of us.

JAN. Old Bear.

AUSTIN. Hm. You know how he got that name? *(***JAN** *looks up and shakes her head.)* The way I get it, Mrs. Lori, your grandmother, tried to teach him to dance.

JAN. Pawpaw could dance?

AUSTIN. Uhm, not really. Well, not at first. And Mrs. Lori told him he lumbered around like an old bear in the woods. Well, he just hooted, you know what a laugh he had.

JAN. Yeah.

AUSTIN. *(Smiles.)* He thought that was just grand. And she called him 'Bear' after that.

JAN. I never heard that. Perfect nickname for him.

AUSTIN. Yeah. *(He remembers.)* You should've heard what he called me.

JAN. I still can't believe it.

AUSTIN. It always takes time, hon. Life is full of meetings and partings; that is the way of it. *(***JAN** *looks up at him.)* I saw that in a movie about Scrooge.

JAN. *(sits up.)* Mm. How's Mom?

AUSTIN. She's taking it pretty hard. *(Just then* **BRENDA** *enters through the SL door, sobbing loudly.)* Buuuuut, not as hard as your Aunt Brenda.

BRENDA. *(Between sobs.)* He was such a wonderful, happy man.

(DALE *enters through the door and tries to comfort her.*)

DALE. Shug, you were always arguing with the man.

BRENDA. That doesn't mean I didn't love him!

DALE. I didn't say that.

BRENDA. Well, what DID you say?

DALE. Nothing, I didn't say a thing. (*He shoves his hands into his pants pockets and, looking at* AUSTIN, *shrugs.*)

BRENDA. It just won't be the same... now that he's gone. (*She begins sobbing again.*)

(VAL *enters from the kitchen.*)

AUSTIN. Go ahead, Brenda, let it all out.

DALE. *(to* BRENDA.*)* Yeah, let it all out.

BRENDA. I'm okay, I'll be fine. (*She sniffs loudly and takes a martyr-like stance.*)

DALE. That's my girl. (*He tries to hug her again and she looks at him and begins crying even louder.*) That's it! (*He moves to the recliner and plops down in it.*)

VAL. (*Moves to* BRENDA.) Why don't you go lie down, Bren? I'll bring you a damp cloth.

BRENDA. At least... at least you got to see him. At least one of us was there with him on his last night.

(VAL *forces a smile and then looks away.*)

VAL. Yeah, that was a good thing all right.

BRENDA. I'll... *(sniff)* ...I'll go help Mary Jo. (*She moves to the kitchen door and looks back.*) I'm not totally helpless, you know! (*She exits.*)

DALE. No, but it's a photo-finish!

AUSTIN. Val, you're been such a help to Mary Jo. And we really appreciate your going to see Pawpaw while we went out to dinner.

VAL. Uh... can I talk to you?

AUSTIN. Sure. (*He rises and he and* VAL *move DSL.*)

DALE. I never know what to do or say at times like these.

JAN. Me, either.

DALE. Yeah, but I'm SUPPOSED to say something comforting… something…

AUSITN *(Quietly, to* **VAL.***)* What is it?

VAL. Not sure how to say this. But I have to tell SOMEone. That night – the one you and Mary Jo went out and I said I would go see Dad?

AUSTIN. Yeah?

VAL. I didn't.

AUSTIN. Didn't what?

VAL. I didn't go see him. *(***AUSTIN** *looks at her in surprise.)* Well? Mitchell came in and we talked! And then I,… well, I had a late date and the time sort of –

(Just then **MITCHELL** *enters through the front door.)*

MITCHELL. Reverend Pike said one more time that if there was anything he could do –

DALE. I didn't think he'd EVER leave.

MITCHELL. Where's Mom?

JAN. In the kitchen. Listen, what happened between you and Tish?

MITCHELL. Jan, we can talk about that later.

*(***JAN** *rises and moves to* **MITCHELL.***)*

AUSTIN. *(To* **VAL.***)* Look, maybe later you can tell Mary Jo and Brenda –

VAL. How? I feel SO guilty.

JAN. But I really liked her!

MITCHELL. Well, sometimes these things don't always work out, just because we'd like them to.

DALE. Austin, what're you going to do with all Pawpaw's stuff?

JAN. What? *(She turns to* **AUSTIN.***)* We're not going to get rid of it, are we? *(She runs over to him.)*

AUSTIN. Of course not.

JAN. You can put it all in my room, I don't mind.

AUSTIN. *(Arm around* **JAN.***)* We'll keep it, don't worry. Everything always stays in the family.

DALE. I guess when you get to be his age all you have is a trunk full of keepsakes.

VAL. Where IS his trunk, anyway?

(**AUSTIN** *shoots her a dirty look.*)

AUSTIN. I don't know.

JAN. Wait. (*She looks around.*) Where's Charlemaine? Aunt Brenda didn't let that thing loose in my room again, did she? (*She rushes to the SL door.*) Not again! (*She exits.*)

AUSTIN. Last time I saw that dog it was running down the hall and – OUR ROOM! (*He also bolts out the SL door.*)

MITCHELL. Aunt Val, how're you holding up?

VAL. Oh, fine, I guess. I mean, you think you're prepared for something like this and then when it really DOES happen –

MITCHELL. It's never like you think it would be.

VAL. Nope, it never is.

MITCHELL. (*Puts an arm around her.*) At least, you got to see him one last time. (**VAL** *looks at him and begins to cry! Pulling a handkerchief out of her coat she covers her face.* **MITCHELL** *looks at* **DALE**.) What did I say?

DALE. Boy, are YOU asking the wrong guy.

MITCHELL. (*To* **VAL**.) Here. Just sit here. (*He moves her to the couch.*)

(**MARY JO** *and* **BRENDA** *enter from the kitchen.*)

MARY JO. Do we have to talk about this right now?

BRENDA. I just said I would like some of Dad's things. (**VAL** *stops crying and looks over at her sisters.*) One or two of his old hats, nothing much.

DALE. We were just talking about that.

BRENDA. Oh, what do YOU know?

DALE. Now what was the matter with that?! (*To* **MITCHELL**.) I put two words together and I get jumped on or else somebody start crying.

MARY JO. We can all go through Dad's things and pick out what we'd each like.

BRENDA. Okay, but we have to be fair about it.

MARY JO. Of course. However, Val should have the first choice.

BRENDA. Val? Why does SHE get first choice?

MARY JO. Because, unlike the rest of us, SHE thought enough of him to make sure his last night was spent with the family.

(VAL's eyes get large as she looks out. She rises.)

VAL. Uh, Mary Jo –

MARY JO. No, I insist, Val. We were all thinking of ourselves and you –

BRENDA. Wait just one second there. Are you saying I was being selfish?!

(The others all look at each other; nobody knows how to answer this one. **DALE** *finally throws up his hands and gets out of the chair.)*

DALE. Well, it might as well be me – I haven't said anything right in three weeks. *(He moves to* **BRENDA.***)* Yes, you were being selfish!

BRENDA. How DARE you say that to me! That's not true! *(She looks at the others.)* Is it? *(She looks back, defiantly, at* **DALE.** *However, her smug expression slowly vanishes as she hears no one speak up. She then looks at* **MARY JO** *and* **VAL.***)* Well?

MARY JO. Brenda, you know we all love you –

DALE. But –

MARY JO. We grew up together and nobody is closer than three sisters –

DALE. But –

MARY JO. We're been with you through everything that's ever happened in your life –

DALE. But –

MARY JO. But, yes, you can be very selfish.

(A very uncomfortable silence lands on the room like a Sumo wrestler. **BRENDA** *sniffs haughtily and then sits gently on the couch and stares out.)*

BRENDA. I see.

DALE. *(Points to* **MARY JO.***)* And the ball's in YOUR court!

MARY JO. This is not the time to go through this.

VAL. Mary Jo's right.

BRENDA. *(Imitating* **VAL.***)* 'Mary Jo's right, Mary Jo's right.' You ALWAYS side with her.

VAL. *(Moves to* **BRENDA.***)* I do NOT always side with Mary Jo.

MARY JO. Can we all try to remember what we're all here for?

BRENDA. Yeah. To talk about how selfish Brenda is.

MARY JO. *(sits next to* **BRENDA.***)* We don't talk about that, we never have.

MITCHELL. *(Almost to himself.)* We don't really talk about anything.

MARY JO. *(Looks at* **MITCHELL.***)* Now that's not true, either!

MITCHELL. Oh, sorry! Did you hear that?

VAL. And I do NOT always take Mary Jo's side.

BRENDA. You do so!

MARY JO. That's about true, Val – you and I never argue.

VAL. We do SO!

MARY JO. We do NOT!

*(***AUSTIN*** enters through the SL door.)*

VAL. Well, I'm SORRY!

BRENDA. And you SHOULD be!

VAL. Sorry about THIS?! Well, in THAT case, I'm NOT sorry!

MARY JO. Will you leave Val alone?

BRENDA. And now you're taking HER side!

(The sisters all fold their arms and look out. **AUSTIN** *turns to* **VAL.***)*

AUSTIN. Oh, you finally told them you didn't go see Pawpaw after all?

*(***BRENDA*** and* **MARY JO**'s *eyes widen as they slowly turn to* **VAL.** **VAL** *turns to* **AUSTIN.***)*

MARY JO & BRENDA. WHAT?!

VAL. *(Plaintively, to* **AUSTIN.***)* No, I haven't.

AUSTIN. *(Embarrassed.)* Oh.

DALE. Such is my world and welcome to it.

    *(***MARY JO** *and* **BRENDA** *rise from the couch.)*

MARY JO. You DIDN'T go see Dad?

BRENDA. And let us believe that you did?

VAL. I was going to tell you!

MARY JO. Wait!

BRENDA. *(To* **MARY JO.***)* And SHE's your favorite.

MARY JO. She is NOT my favorite!

VAL. *(Surprised.)* I'm not? *(***MARY JO** *turns to her.)* I'll shut up.

MARY JO. Look, it doesn't make any difference.

BRENDA. But –

MARY JO. We ALL could've gone to see him that night… but we didn't. And arguing won't change that.

AUSTIN. Can I say something?

VAL. Will you check with me first? *(She moves to the couch and sits.)*

DALE. This is the touchiest family.

    (The doorbell rings.)

MITCHELL. Now who? *(He moves to the front door.)*

AUSTIN. I spoke with Dr. Parnell. And I don't think it would've made any difference if we HAD gone to see him.

MARY JO. Oh, what does that mean?

    *(***MITCHELL** *opens the front door and* **TISH** *enters, carrying a covered dish.)*

MITCHELL. *(Surprised.)* Tish! What're you… come in!

TISH. Hello. I… I heard about Pawpaw. I – well, I brought a casserole. You're supposed to bring casseroles, aren't you?

MARY JO. *(Moves to* **TISH.***)* Thanks you, dear. That's so nice of you. *(She takes the dish.)*

MITCHELL. How'd you know? I mean, about Pawpaw?

TISH. I got a phone call.

MITCHELL. Oh! *(He moves to the SL door.)* I know who it was who called, too. *(He calls out.)* Jan?! Jan!

TISH. No.

MITCHELL. She was so excited about getting to be in the wedding.

TISH. She didn't call me.

MITCHELL. Well, if she didn't who did?

MARY JO. I called her.

(Everyone in the room turns and look at MARY JO.)

BRENDA. You? You called HER?

AUSTIN. I'm proud of you, dear.

MITCHELL. Mom? You called Tish?

(JAN enters through the SL door.)

JAN. What?

MITCHELL. Sorry. I was going to accuse you of something.

JAN. *(Reflex.)* I didn't do it.

MITCHELL. No, turns out you didn't.

JAN. *(Amazed.)* You mean that works?

MITCHELL. Mom did. *(He moves to MARY JO.)* You called Tish?

MARY JO. Yes, I did. You see – *(She look at AUSTIN)* – I thought I'd stick my nose in here.

AUSTIN. *(Hands up.)* No complaints from me.

MITCHELL. But we broke up! *(He sheepishly looks at TISH.)* Well, we did.

MARY JO. Yes, because she thinks you're too much of a 'mamma's boy.'

MITCHELL. How did you know that?

TISH. I told her. *(MITCHELL turns to her.)* She ASKED!

MARY JO. *(Holds out the casserole.)* Will somebody take this?

AUSTIN. *(Moves to MARY JO.)* I got it. *(He takes the dish from her and hands it to JAN.)* Put this in the kitchen.

JAN. 'I got it', he says. *(She moves to the kitchen door.)* What would this family do without me? *(She exits into the kitchen.)*

MARY JO. Yes, I did ask her. See, I thought it was time we finally had that talk we kept putting off. In fact, it was me who kept putting it off.

MITCHELL. Well, it's all right with me… *(He turns to **TISH**.)* If it's all right with you?

TISH. I'm here, aren't I?

MITCHELL. Yes, you are. *(He takes her hand.)* And thank you. *(They hug.)*

TISH. How are you? Are you all right?

MITCHELL. I'm okay. *(They snuggle a bit.)*

TISH. I know how close you were to Pawpaw. He seemed like such a nice man.

MITCHELL. Oh, he was. *(He looks at the others.)* And we all miss him so much. We may SHOW it in different ways… but it all means the same thing.

VAL. That's true. *(She turns to **BRENDA**.)* Sorry I said you were selfish.

BRENDA. Oh, you didn't really say that.

DALE. Yes, she did.

VAL & BRENDA. *(To **DALE**.)* Shut up!

*(The phone rings. **AUSTIN** moves to the desk and picks up the receiver.)*

BRENDA. You're the reason we're not in our own house right now.

DALE. Hey, we can argue just as well here as there.

AUSTIN. Hello. No, this is the Rogers house. Oh! Yes, he is. Just a second. *(He holds out the receiver.)* Dale.

DALE. You mean somebody WANTS to talk to me?

AUSTIN. Get over here. *(**DALE** moves to **AUSTIN**.)* I think it's your insurance guy.

DALE. Oh, that makes the day perfect. *(Takes the receiver.)* Hello? *(He turns his back on the others as he continues the phone call.)*

TISH. Mrs. Rogers, I never REALLY thought Mitch is a momma's boy.

MITCHELL. Then why did you say it?

TISH. Because you got me so mad!

MITCHELL. About what?

(TISH stares at him but cannot remember.)

TISH. Well,… it'll come to me.

(JAN enters through the kitchen door.)

MARY JO. That's what I thought. *(To MITCHELL.)* And you can't remember, either, right?

MITCHELL. Not really, no.

MARY JO. Uh huh. A lot of arguments are over nothing. And later nobody remembers what they were arguing about in the first place.

BRENDA. I remember what Dale and I were arguing about!

VAL. You remember what you and I were arguing about on your ninth birthday.

BRENDA. I should've gotten to ride on the pony first; it was MY birthday!

VAL. Here we go!

DALE. *(Into the receiver.)* Thank you. SO much. I'll get back to you. Right. Bye. *(He hangs up the phone and saunters over to BRENDA.)* Lah de dah de dah de dah.

AUSTIN. What was that all about, Miss Scarlett?

BRENDA. Let me guess. Our insurance company is dropping us. You missed a payment, right?

DALE. Wrong, my little coronary. Our ever-watchful and diligent insurance company just heard from the fire department. About the fire? Turns out it was NOT caused by any of my cigars.

BRENDA. Yeah? Then what?

DALE. *(He leans in to her.)* It was caused by a short in an electrical appliance. *(He leans in to BRENDA.)* It SEEMS that SOMEbody left the hair dryer plugged in.

(**BRENDA** *starts to speak defiantly, then turns away, now embarrassed.*)

BRENDA. *(Quietly.)* Oh.

DALE. *(To* **AUSTIN***.)* And one other thing. *(He tries to laugh this off.)* We had complete coverage in a case such as this… which includes money for our hotel… if we stayed in a hotel during the… the uh… rebuilding of the damaged sections… of the uh… the house.

BRENDA. So we could've stayed in a hotel.

JAN. *(Happily.)* I'll get the dog.

MARY JO. Just a second.

BRENDA. Sorry, Mary Jo, I had no idea –

MARY JO. Why are you apologizing? So you stayed with us a few days? Isn't that what families do? And we are a family, you know.

BRENDA. I… I guess.

AUSTIN. *(Realizes.)* Hair dryer! *(He bolts out the SL door.)*

JAN. *(to* **AUSTIN** *as he exits.)* Get the dog!

DALE. We'll be out tonight, Mary Jo. I'll get the suitcases packed and –

MARY JO. No sense in your leaving now and trying to find a hotel in the middle of the night. You'll wait until tomorrow. (**DALE** *starts to speak.*) And that's that.

VAL. Pawpaw would've wanted it that way.

BRENDA. That's probably true. And we can go over what items we each want of his.

VAL. Yeah, his keepsakes, as he called them.

JAN. Keepsakes?

MARY JO. Oh, I know. Another old phrase.

JAN. No, what are keepsakes?

(**MARY JO** *looks at her and then at the others. She then puts an arm around* **JAN**.)

MARY JO. You. You are a keepsake. *(Again she looks at the others.)* We are all keepsakes; that's what a family is, isn't it? We go through one thing after another, some bad – *(He moves to* **MITCHELL** *and hugs him)* – and some good. *(She looks at the others.)* But we keep the family together.

VAL. I never looked at it that way.

BRENDA. *(Trying to lighten the mood.)* Read that in some magazine?

MARY JO. *(Smiling.)* No. I just made it up.

BRENDA. Well, maybe we can send it in somewhere.

MARY JO. *(Kidding back.)* Oh, you think?

*(***AUSTIN** *enters through the SL door.)*

AUSTIN. Everything's unplugged.

MITCHELL. That's a good scout. Hey, I got an idea. While everyone's here… I have the camera in the car.

DALE. You want to take a picture? Now?

MITCHELL. I mean we have everyone together? And we've all hosed off and dressed up and everything.

AUSTIN. Good idea, son. Go get it.

MITCHELL. Got a man on it.

TISH. I'll help you.

MITCHELL. I thought you'd never volunteer.

DALE. You never volunteer.

*(***MITCHELL** *and* **TISH** *exit out the front door.* **MARY JO** *moves to the door and looks out.* **AUSTIN** *moves to her.)*

AUSTIN. I'm glad you finally like her.

MARY JO. I always liked her. *(The others exchange looks.* **MARY JO** *moves to the couch.)* Well, I do.

VAL. I still feel so guilty. About not being with Dad? *(***MARY JO** *nods.)*

AUSTIN. Because he didn't have any family around him that last night? *(The others look at him.)* Well, that's not really true. Not from his view, anyway.

JAN. Huh?

MARY JO. Austin, we didn't go, Brenda didn't go, Val –

AUSTIN. Wait. I told you I spoke with Dr. Parnell. He said that while there were nurses there with him off and on, Pawpaw spent most of his time not talking to them.

DALE. NOT talking to them?

AUSTIN. No. He spent his time talking to someone else. *(MARY JO looks at him curiously.)* Hon, he was talking to Mrs. Lori.

JAN. Gramma?

VAL. What did he say?

AUSTIN. Well, they didn't quote him – just said he kept talking with her. *(He puts an arm around MARY JO's waist.)* And apparently she was talking with him.

BRENDA. You're not going to stand there and tell us that some ghost –

MARY JO. No. It doesn't matter. It's what HE saw. *(He looks at AUSTIN.)* He wasn't alone after all.

AUSTIN. The Doc said something about Pawpaw apologizing that he couldn't dance with her. At least, not right then.

VAL. You're not making all this up, are you, Austin?

AUSTIN. *(Hand up as if taking an oath.)* Call Dr. Parnell if you don't believe me.

(MITCHELL and TISH enter carrying the camera, attached to a tripod.)

MITCHELL. Okay, everybody over to the couch.

MARY JO. Right. *(She and the others move to the couch, as MITCHELL sets up the tripod DSC, aiming the camera at the couch.)* Let's put us sisters on the couch.

VAL. Okay. *(She sits on one side of the couch and BRENDA sits on the other.)*

AUSTIN. Men in the back. *(He moves behind the couch.)*

DALE. Where else. *(He moves next to AUSTIN.)*

AUSTIN. Jan? Lean on the couch arm there.

(JAN moves to the SR couch arm and faces the camera.)

MARY JO. Tish?

TISH. What?

MARY JO. Get in the picture.

(TISH is hesitant until MITCHELL nudges her.)

MITCHELL. Go on. Other couch arm.

TISH. *(Smiling.)* Okay. *(She moves to the other couch arm.)*

MITCHELL. Let me adjust the lights. *(He turns off one of the wall switches next to the front door and all the LIGHTS near the door, SR, go out, highlighting the area around the couch.)* There, that's better.

MARY JO. Wait!

MITCHELL. What?

MARY JO. *(Point to the desk.)* Pawpaw's picture!

MITCHELL. Oh! *(He moves to the desk.)* Good idea. *(He picks up PAWPAW's framed photo and hands it to his mother.)* Just hold that and face it just at this angle.

MARY JO. *(Holding the picture.)* Like ths?

MITCHELL. *(Moving back to the camera.)* That way it won't glare. *(He adjusts the camera and stands upright.)* Ready? *(He pushes a button and rushes over to stand next to the men behind the couch.)* Now. Don't anybody move!

BRENDA. What about Charlemaine?

MARY JO, VAL & DALE. Don't talk!

(BRENDA freezes, along with the others, facing the camera.

At this moment, a slow Big Band tune fades in. The SR area becomes lit as if by the moon and PAWPAW, now dressed in his best suit, and LORI dance into view. After a few spins on the floor they freeze and the camera flashes.)

(LIGHTS and MUSIC fade out.)

End

PROP LIST

ACT I
A camera and tripod
3 ladies purses
Purse contents (cosmetics, keys, tissues, etc.)
Girl's diary Pen

ACT II
Portable pet carrier
Luggage
Sheets
A pillow

ACT III
Various dirty dishes and glasses
A casserole
A camera and tripod

COSTUMES

Keepsakes is a contemporary show so the costumes should follow this theme. The only exceptions is in **ACT II** where AUSTIN is wearing loud shorts and DALE is wearing loud pajamas. Also, in **ACT III** everyone should be dressed in mourning.

The Committee Meeting

A Comedy for Five Women in One Act
By Joellen K. Bland

5f / interior

Sue and her committee get together to plan the church congregational dinner-meeting. While she tries to guide the discussion - often with the aid of a whistle to restore order - Amy prattles, Edith complains, Doris preaches and Mary amiably agrees with just about everything. They willingly offer comments, ideas and suggestions, but when they are asked to assume responsibility, each responds with a prompt excuse for not accepting, and volunteers the time and services of someone else.

Please visit our website **bakersplays.com** for complete descriptions and licensing information

The Babysitter

Laurie Woodward 5f / interior

Eyes at the window," warns the Ouija board, and Karen realizes that she and her friends are being watched! Searching the house, she discovers there is no child to babysit! An old newspaper clipping reveals that the Williams' baby daughter died mysteriously ten years ago. The terrifying finale reveals who the Williams are, and what is in store for the babysitter! A thriller for all lovers of things that go bump in the night!

Please visit our website **bakersplays.com** for complete descriptions and licensing information

The Strange Charm of a Good Legacy
by Mindy Mayer

Drama, 2M, 5W

"Was it real, a dream, or just a regret?" Loss, legacy and lore all play a role as the story, set in New Orleans, moves from present to past. Olivia, now in her late sixties, lost her dream of becoming a partner in the family coffee company when she was a teenager. All that remains a half century later are memories of a more elegant life and the family estate, which her daughter Valerie, is now pressuring her to sell. A disclosure of a family secret of Ann Aimee, Olivia's closest cousin, to Ford, Ann Aimee's first love, resonates fifty years later when they all reunite and reflect on their younger selves. The play takes a sensitive look at the effect of time on love, family and friendship.

Please visit our website
bakersplays.com
for complete descriptions and licensing information

www.ingramcontent.com/pod-product-compliance
Lightning Source LLC
Chambersburg PA
CBHW071841290426
44109CB00017B/1889